London Unveiled:

A Traveler's Guide To The Heart Of The Uk | History, Culture, And Iconic Experiences Await

Artemis Pendlebrook

© Copyright 2024 - All rights reserved.

The contents of this book may not be reproduced, duplicated, or transmitted without the direct written permission of the author or publisher.

Under no circumstances will the publisher or author be held liable for any damages, recovery, or financial loss due to the information contained in this book. Neither directly nor indirectly.

Legal Notice:

This book is protected by copyright. This book is for personal use only. You may not modify, distribute, sell, use, quote, or paraphrase any part or content of this book without the permission of the author or publisher.

Disclaimer Notice:

Please note that the information contained in this document is for educational and entertainment purposes only. Every effort has been made to present accurate, current, reliable, and complete information. No warranties of any kind are stated or implied. The reader acknowledges that the author is not offering legal, financial, medical, or professional advice. The contents of this book have been taken from various sources. Please consult a licensed professional before attempting any of the techniques described in this book.

By reading this document, the reader agrees that under no circumstances will the author be liable for any direct or indirect loss arising from the use of the information contained in this document, including but not limited to - errors, omissions, or inaccuracies.

Table of Contents

Chapter 1 Introduction to London 5

Overview of London's Rich History 5

The Cultural Melting Pot: London's Diversity 6

Getting Around: Transportation Tips 8

Weather and Best Times to Visit 9

Essential Travel Information: Currency, Language, and Safety Tips 11

Chapter 2 Iconic Landmarks and Historical Sites 14

Buckingham Palace: The Royal Residence 14

Tower of London: A Historic Fortress 17

The British Museum: Treasures from Around the World 19

Westminster Abbey: A Symbol of British Tradition 21

St. Paul's Cathedral: Architectural Splendor 23

Chapter 3 Neighborhood Exploration 26

Soho: London's Entertainment Hub 26

Notting Hill: Quaint Streets and Colorful Markets 28

Camden Town: Alternative Culture and Markets 30

Shoreditch: Trendy Art and Street Food Scene 32

Greenwich: Maritime History and Greenwich Mean Time 34

Chapter 4 Parks and Outdoor Activities 37

Hyde Park: Serenity in the Heart of London 37

Regent's Park: A Haven for Nature Lovers 39

Hampstead Heath: Stunning Views and Open Spaces 41

Kensington Gardens: Greenery by the Palaces 43

Thames Path: Riverside Walks and Iconic Views 45

Chapter 5 Culinary Adventures 47

Traditional British Cuisine: Exploring Classics 47

Multicultural London: Global Flavors 49

Borough Market: A Gastronomic Paradise 51

Afternoon Tea: A British Tradition 53

Michelin-Starred Dining: Fine Culinary Experiences 55

Chapter 6 Cultural Experiences 58

West End Shows: London's Theater Scene 58

Museums and Galleries: Art and History 60

Music Scene: From Classical to Contemporary 62

Literary London: Bookish Hotspots 64

Festivals and Events: Celebrating Diversity 66

Chapter 7 Practical Tips and Local Insights 69

Accommodation Options: From Luxury to Budget 69

Navigating Public Transportation 71

Shopping in London: From High-End to Vintage 75

Health and Safety Tips for Travelers 76

Sustainable Travel: Responsible Tourism in London 79

Conclusion 83

A Sustainable Journey through London's Tapestry 83

Chapter 1
Introduction to London

Overview of London's Rich History

With its roots firmly ingrained in historical chronicles, London, the esteemed capital of the United Kingdom, is a monument to the unrelenting passage of time. A winding trip through the city's history provides an engrossing story, with each chapter taking place against the backdrop of its famous skyline and important historical sites.

Around the year 50 AD, the Roman colony of Londinium was established, marking the beginning of London's history. What had started out as a tactical outpost quickly expanded into a thriving commercial hub complete with amphitheaters, temples, and forums. The ruins of the old city walls and the finding of items that narrate stories of trade and culture bear witness to the Roman legacy of Londinium.

The Tower of London rose as a stronghold on the banks of the River Thames, casting a shadow of the Middle Ages over the city. Constructed initially to represent Norman dominance, it subsequently functioned as a royal residence, treasury, and even a jail. Westminster Abbey, with its lofty spires and Gothic design, served as the sacred site for royal coronations, marriages, and the ultimate resting place for kings.

Dramatic events characterized the Middle Ages, from the political intrigues of the War of the Roses to the devastating Black Death that ravaged the city and permanently altered its social and demographic makeup. A major event that cleared the path for the modern restoration of London was the Great Fire of 1666, which destroyed a large portion of the city's medieval architecture.

A time of unparalleled progress and change was ushered in by the Victorian era. The Industrial Revolution began under Queen Victoria's reign, and London became a vibrant center of innovation and trade. Magnificent structures such as the Crystal Palace demonstrated the city's strength, and the vast railway system linked the vast metropolitan area.

London was in the forefront of world events during the 20th century, from the cultural revolution of the Swinging Sixties to the destruction of two World Wars. The city, left in its wake by violence, came to represent resiliency and rebirth. Today, the ruins of buildings destroyed by bombs contrast sharply with modern skyscrapers, forming a history of the city's resilience.

Modern wonders like the London Eye and the Shard mix with historic sites like St. Paul's Cathedral and the Tower Bridge in London's contemporary landscape. A storehouse of human history, the British Museum invites visitors to examine the objects that span thousands of years. A constant companion to the development of the city, the River Thames winds past cultural hotspots and historic attractions to connect the many communities that make up London.

The sounds of centuries past reverberate through the city's winding alleyways, beckoning daring adventurers to immerse themselves in the historical layers that have woven London into the colorful, international tapestry that it is today. London's rich and varied story is told everywhere, from the grand halls of Buckingham Palace to the cobblestone streets of Covent Garden. It is a constant reminder of the city's enduring vitality.

The Cultural Melting Pot: London's Diversity

London is a vast, vibrant city that is a monument to the magnificent blending of cultures that has shaped its very character. The city's colorful tapestry is woven with diverse threads, resulting in a cultural mosaic that enthralls and honors the wide range of influences that converge within its boundaries.

The story of diversity in London starts with the flood of immigrants that came to the city because of its opportunity and magnetic appeal. These people came from all over the world. Waves of migration have molded London's neighborhoods, customs, and very essence over the ages, creating a distinct character that is global in scope.

London's streets are a monument to the peaceful coexistence of cultures from all over the world. Vibrant Afro-Caribbean influences abound in neighborhoods like Brixton, from the lively markets to the sounds of live music flowing from nearby establishments. Chinatown transports visitors to the heart of East Asia with its elaborate gates and fragrant passageways while providing a mouthwatering assortment of culinary delights and cultural events.

In places like Brick Lane, where the walls are covered in colorful street art and the air is filled with the fragrances of spices, the South Asian diaspora has left a lasting impression. In the meantime, the warmth of Italian hospitality and the perfume of freshly made espresso beckon in Soho's Little Italy.

Beyond racial and cultural divides, London's diversity embraces a wide range of LGBTQ+ populations. With its well-known rainbow crosswalks, Soho is a central location for the LGBTQ+ community, providing a wide range of pubs, clubs, and welcoming areas that perfectly capture London's values of inclusion and individualism.

Cultural establishments like the British Museum and the Tate Modern present an international collection of artwork and artifacts, demonstrating the city's commitment to promoting intercultural understanding. Notting Hill Carnival, Chinese New Year, and Diwali festivals light up the city with a riot of color, music, and dance, enticing everyone to join in the happy celebrations.

London has a diverse population, but it also has a diverse food, fashion, and linguistic scene. You may find a gastronomic kaleidoscope when you stroll through the busy markets on Borough or Portobello Road, ranging from classic British fare to unique international treats. The city's reputation as a global trendsetter is reflected in the unique mix of styles found in fashion districts such as Carnaby Street and Brick Lane.

The symphony of languages spoken in this melting pot of cultures is evidence of the city's multiculturalism. London is more than simply a place; it is a vibrant, living example of unity in diversity, where the collision of cultures has not only been welcomed but has also grown into a harmonious fusion that embodies the city's essence. London is a lighthouse that welcomes everyone into its embrace and incorporates their tales into the rich tapestry of its diverse and dynamic personality, from the busy markets to the peaceful nooks of its neighborhoods.

Getting Around: Transportation Tips

Getting around the complex transit network in London is essential to experiencing the vibrant pulse of the city. London's famous red double-decker buses, black taxis, and extensive Underground system provide visitors with a wide range of ways to move through the city's busy streets.

London Underground (The Tube): The heartbeat of London's transportation, the Underground, or "Tube," is a vast network of trains connecting every corner of the city. With color-coded lines and a comprehensive map, it's the fastest way to travel between neighborhoods. Oyster cards or contactless payment methods are your ticket to hassle-free journeys, providing a cost-effective and efficient means of payment.

Buses: The recognizable red buses of London serve as both a means of transit and a visual landmark. Buses are a practical way to visit locations not served by the Tube because they have a vast network and beautiful routes. Buses accept contactless payment cards and Oyster cards, which eliminate the need for cash.

Black Cabs: When traveling on routes that are not served by public transportation, London's black taxis are a dependable and traditional means of transportation. Black taxis are easily hailed on the street and are operated by skilled drivers who have completed extensive training, guaranteeing a quick and safe ride. Even though this choice is a little more expensive than others, the comfort and convenience usually make it worthwhile.

Dockless Bikes: For the eco-conscious traveler, London's cycle hire scheme provides an opportunity to explore the city at a leisurely pace. Dockless bikes, conveniently available at numerous locations, offer a healthy and environmentally friendly alternative for short trips within the city.

River Services: The majestic River Thames serves as a scenic highway through the heart of London. River bus services and commuter boats provide a unique perspective of the city's landmarks while offering an alternative mode of transportation, particularly useful for those along the riverbanks.

Overground Trains: London's Overground trains efficiently connect neighborhoods outside of the city center to outlying locations. These trains, which are completely integrated into the Oyster card system, expand the reach of public transit and provide a simple way to explore the city's various areas.

Travel Apps: Numerous travel applications offer real-time data on public transportation timetables, delays, and other routes to help you travel more efficiently. You can explore the city with ease with the help of apps like Citymapper and TfL (Transport for London), which can be helpful companions.

Whether by Tube, bus, black cab, or a leisurely bike ride, London's transportation system is a well-orchestrated symphony, ensuring that every traveler can explore the city comfortably and efficiently. Embrace the diversity of options available, and you'll find that getting around in London becomes an integral part of your immersive experience in this vibrant metropolis.

Weather and Best Times to Visit

London's weather, though famously unpredictable, adds an element of charm to the city's diverse experiences. The best time to visit depends on your preferences, as each season in London brings its own unique appeal.

Spring (March to May): Spring paints London with a burst of color as parks and gardens come alive with blossoms. Mild temperatures, ranging from 50°F to 65°F (10°C to 18°C), make it an ideal time for outdoor exploration. Parks such as Hyde Park and Kew Gardens offer a picturesque setting, and cultural events often flourish during this season.

Summer (June to August): Summer is peak tourist season, and for good reason. With longer days and temperatures averaging between 60°F to 75°F (15°C to 24°C), London basks in a lively atmosphere. Parks host picnics and outdoor events, while festivals and open-air concerts dot the city's cultural calendar. Be prepared for crowds, and book accommodations and attractions in advance.

Autumn (September to November): London wraps itself in an autumnal tapestry as summer draws to an end. With cool temps between 50°F and 65°F (10°C and 18°C), it's a great time to explore sans the summer crowds. Parks become a riot of reds and golds, and if there are sporadic downpours, indoor attractions provide relief.

Winter (December to February): With holiday lights illuminating the city, winter in London is a lovely time of year. Even though it's between 30°F and 45°F (-1°C and 7°C), the festive atmosphere makes the streets feel warm. Enchanting experiences may be found at Somerset House's ice rink, Hyde Park's Winter Wonderland, and the city's Christmas markets. Invest on warm clothing and enjoy cosy times at classic pubs.

Best Times to Visit: Late spring (May) to early October is usually the best time to visit London (September). The pleasant weather and prime time for outdoor attractions coincide with this period. But if you'd rather be alone and don't mind the odd downpour, late fall (October) can be a great time.

Tips for Weather Readiness:

- **Layered Clothing:** Given the changeable weather, bring layers to adapt to temperature shifts.
- **Umbrella:** A compact umbrella is a handy companion for unexpected drizzles.

- **Comfortable Shoes:** London's charm lies in its walkable neighborhoods, so comfortable shoes are a must.
- **Weather Apps:** Stay informed with weather apps to plan your daily excursions accordingly.

Whether under the gentle bloom of spring, the warmth of summer, the colors of autumn, or the festive glow of winter, London welcomes visitors year-round. Each season unfolds a unique facet of the city's character, ensuring that there's never a dull moment in this vibrant metropolis.

Essential Travel Information: Currency, Language, and Safety Tips

The British Pound Sterling (£), which is extensively used across the city, is the official currency of London. £5, £10, £20, and £50 are the denominations of banknotes; coins have the following denominations: £2, £1, 50p, 20p, 10p, 5p, 2p, and 1p. There are lots of ATMs that take most debit and credit cards. Although banks, exchange bureaus, and airports offer currency exchange services, using ATMs to withdraw cash is frequently more economical.

Language: Since English is the language used by most people in London, especially those employed in the service sector, most people speak it fluently. But because the city is multicultural, you may run into people who speak other languages, which reflects the wide range of backgrounds that the city's citizens come from. Information, announcements on public transportation, and official signage are all in English.

Safety Tips:

1. Public Transport Awareness:
   - While using public transportation, particularly in crowded areas such as the Tube or buses, remain vigilant to protect your belongings from pickpockets.
   - Be cautious with valuables and keep an eye on your belongings at tourist attractions and in crowded markets.
2. Emergency Services:

- In case of emergencies, dial 999 for immediate assistance from police, ambulance, or fire services. For non-emergencies, you can contact the police at 101.
- If you need medical attention, the National Health Service (NHS) provides emergency medical services, and it's recommended to have travel insurance covering healthcare expenses for non-urgent situations.

3. Healthcare:
   - Familiarize yourself with the location of hospitals and medical facilities in the areas you plan to visit.
   - Ensure you have any necessary medications and know where to find pharmacies.

4. Traffic Safety:
   - Remember that traffic moves on the left side of the road in the UK. Look right first when crossing the street.
   - Use designated pedestrian crossings, especially in busy areas, and be aware of cyclists and buses.

5. Cultural Sensitivity:
   - London is known for its cultural diversity, and it's important to be respectful of various customs and traditions.
   - Dress modestly when visiting religious sites, and be mindful of local customs to ensure a positive cultural experience.

6. Weather Preparedness:
   - London's weather can be unpredictable, so it's advisable to carry an umbrella and dress in layers.
   - Stay informed about weather forecasts, especially during the colder months, and plan accordingly.

7. Local Laws and Customs:
   - Familiarize yourself with local laws, including those related to smoking, drinking in public places, and littering.
   - Smoking is prohibited on public transport, in enclosed public spaces, and in many outdoor areas.

8. Transportation Safety:
   - When using taxis, ensure they are licensed. Recognizable black cabs and licensed minicabs are safe options. Ride-sharing services like Uber are also widely available.
   - Follow safety guidelines when using public transport, and use reputable transportation options to ensure a secure and comfortable journey.

Remember to stay updated on travel advisories and remain aware of your surroundings. London is generally a safe city for tourists, and by practicing common-sense precautions, you can enjoy your visit to this vibrant and welcoming metropolis with peace of mind.

Chapter 2
Iconic Landmarks and Historical Sites

Buckingham Palace: The Royal Residence

Buckingham Palace, an iconic symbol of British royalty and grandeur, stands proudly at the heart of London, radiating regal elegance and historical significance. As the official residence of the reigning monarch, it has been a focal point of the monarchy since the accession of Queen Victoria in 1837.

1. Architectural Grandeur:

- Built as a townhouse for the Duke of Buckingham in 1703, Buckingham Palace experienced extensive repairs and additions in the early 1800s, overseen by architect John Nash. Shining with Portland stone, the façade harmoniously blends French Empire and Neoclassical architectural forms to create a building that is strong and graceful at the same time.
- The famous balcony of the palace, which was erected in the 20th century, has been crucial to several historical moments. Notably,

the Royal Family congregates there for public appearances and greetings at important events like royal weddings and national holidays.

2. Changing of the Guard:

- The Buckingham Palace Changing of the Guard event is a painstakingly planned demonstration of military tradition and accuracy. The Queen's Guard, which consists of troops from the Foot Guards regiments, performs the ceremony with great care and attention to detail, drawing large audiences who are anxious to see this famous show.
- The Guards provide a visual spectacle that symbolizes the rich history and ceremonial magnificence associated with the British monarchy as they march to the beat of military music while wearing their characteristic red tunics, bearskin helmets, and polished black boots.

3. State Rooms and Gardens:

- The State Rooms open for business throughout the summer, letting guests experience Buckingham Palace's lavish decor. Exquisite artwork, rare antiques, and opulent furnishings are displayed in the lavishly decorated State Rooms, which include the Throne Room, the Grand Ballroom, and the White Drawing Room. These rooms attest to the palace's importance in hosting dignitaries and state ceremonies.
- The 39 acres of well-kept gardens offer a peaceful haven in the middle of the busy metropolis. The gardens date back to the 1820s and include colorful flower beds, meandering paths, and a gorgeous lake. While touring this verdant sanctuary, guests can admire the careful gardening.

4. Royal Events and Receptions:

- Buckingham Palace is the venue for important royal occasions and festivities. The Ballroom, with its magnificent chandeliers and elaborate décor, has served as the venue for state dinners honoring distinguished guests. The palace's significance in these well-

- publicized occasions enhances its reputation as a representation of tradition and continuity in the British monarchy.
- Formal gatherings within the palace gates offer insight into the complex traditions and etiquette surrounding diplomatic encounters, demonstrating the monarchy's continuing significance in both ceremonial and diplomatic contexts.

5. The Victoria Memorial:

- A masterpiece unto itself, the Victoria Memorial stands conspicuously in front of Buckingham Palace. A gilded statue of Queen Victoria sits atop a stately marble structure decorated with bronze figures and allegorical sculptures, all part of the memorial designed by sculptor Sir Thomas Brock. The ensemble honors the second-longest reigning king in British history and was finished in 1911.
- Beautifully designed gardens envelop the memorial, offering a tasteful precursor to the opulence of Buckingham Palace and a well-liked location for residents and visitors to take in the scenery.

Visiting Tips:

- Consider taking one of the guided tours of Buckingham Palace for a more immersive experience. These tours include extensive information on the palace's history, design, and royal family life.
- The Queen's Gallery, housed within Buckingham Palace, provides art enthusiasts with an opportunity to examine the variety of treasures held by the queen through revolving exhibitions of the Royal Collection.
- Consider visiting Buckingham Palace during the day to admire its architectural intricacies and returning in the evening to see the façade lit up against the night sky in order to capture the essence of the building in various lighting conditions.

Buckingham Palace, with its architectural splendor, ceremonial traditions, and historical significance, stands as an enduring symbol of the British monarchy. Beyond its role as a royal residence, it beckons visitors to immerse themselves in the cultural legacy and grandeur associated with one of the world's most iconic palaces.

Tower of London: A Historic Fortress

The Tower of London, a monumental fortress that has stood sentry over the River Thames for over a millennium, is a living testament to the rich tapestry of British history. Originally conceived as a symbol of power and control, this historic complex has played multifaceted roles over the centuries, evolving from a military stronghold to a royal palace, and eventually, a treasury and prison.

1. Architectural Marvel:

- Established in 1066 by William the Conqueror, the Tower of London is a formidable representation of Norman military construction. The primary keep, the White Tower, made a powerful statement of control and strength with its strong walls and commanding presence.
- The Inner and Outer Ward, the famous Tower Bridge, and the medieval Chapel of St. Peter ad Vincula were among the new buildings added to the complex by later kings, including as Richard the Lionheart and Henry III.

2. Royal Palace and Prison:

- The Tower has seen a wide range of significant historical occurrences, including serving as a monarch's home. Notably, from Henry III to Elizabeth I, it was the preferred home of

monarchs. Its lavish chambers, like Wakefield Tower from the Middle Ages, offer an insight into the royal family's affluent way of life.
- Along with being a legendary jail, the Tower's grim past was entwined with stories of nobles like Anne Boleyn, Lady Jane Grey, and Thomas More who were imprisoned. The prisoner entryway known as the Traitors' Gate is still eerie reminder of the terrible past of the Tower.

3. Crown Jewels and Treasury:

- The Crown Jewels, a glittering assortment of regalia that includes the renowned Koh-i-Noor diamond, the Imperial State Crown, and the Sovereign's Orb, are kept at the Tower of London. Watched over by the Yeoman Warders, or Beefeaters, these valuable relics are on display in the Jewel House for visitors to gaze over.
- Once the royal mint and treasury, the Martin Tower occupies a large portion of the White Tower. Large amounts of gold and silver were kept there, enhancing the Tower's reputation as a stronghold of riches and stability.

4. Yeoman Warders and Ravens:

- The Yeoman Warders, or Beefeaters, are an integral part of the Tower's history. These ceremonial guardians, distinguished by their traditional uniforms, conduct guided tours that provide engaging insights into the Tower's legends and lore.
- Legend has it that if the resident ravens ever leave the Tower, the kingdom will fall. Today, the Tower maintains a group of ravens, tended to by the Ravenmaster, ensuring the continuity of this quirky and enduring superstition.

5. Tower Green and Executions:

- A peaceful area inside the Tower gates, Tower Green has a somber past filled with political hangings. This was the place where notable people including Anne Boleyn, Catherine Howard, and

Lady Jane Grey met their demise. A memorial honoring individuals who faced the executioner's block marks the location.
- Tower Green presently has an outline of the medieval scaffold site, the scene of numerous notorious beheadings, a gloomy reminder of the Tower's dramatic and sinister past.

Visiting Tips:

- Allow ample time to explore the Tower of London, as its extensive history and numerous attractions can easily fill a day.
- Engage with the Yeoman Warders during their guided tours for a captivating narrative of the Tower's history and anecdotes.
- Visit during off-peak hours or consider guided tours for a more personalized experience.

The Tower of London, with its formidable architecture and layered history, invites visitors to traverse the corridors of time. As a guardian of royal secrets, a seat of power, and a symbol of resilience, the Tower remains a captivating destination that unveils the complexities of Britain's storied past.

The British Museum: Treasures from Around the World

The British Museum, an awe-inspiring repository of human history and culture, stands majestically in the heart of London, inviting visitors on a journey through time and across continents. Established in 1753, this world-renowned institution houses an extensive collection of artifacts that span millennia, offering a profound exploration of the achievements, innovations, and diversity of civilizations from around the globe.

1. Architectural Grandeur:

- Sir Robert Smirke created a magnificent neoclassical building that now houses the British Museum. The famous 44-column Greek Revival façade sets the scene for the colossal treasures within.
- The Great Court, a magnificent area with a glass canopy in the center of the museum, offers a striking focal point and acts as a starting point for guests to go on their cultural tour.

2. Rosetta Stone and Egyptian Collection:

- The Rosetta Stone is one of the most well-known items in the museum and is essential to understanding ancient Egyptian hieroglyphs. Its finding was a turning point in our knowledge of ancient languages.
- Among the best in the world, the Egyptian collection features colossal sculptures, mummies, and the renowned Elgin Marbles from the Parthenon in Athens. It provides an enthralling look at the magnificence of past civilizations.

3. Assyrian Winged Bulls and Mesopotamian Treasures:

- The enormous winged bulls that stand watch over old palaces are on display in the Assyrian galleries. These massive statues, which demonstrate the might of Mesopotamian artistic and military achievement, transport viewers to the powerful Assyrian Empire.
- The Cyrus Cylinder and the Standard of Ur are two examples of Mesopotamian treasures that reveal the accomplishments of prehistoric societies that flourished between the Tigris and Euphrates rivers.

4. Greek and Roman Antiquities:

- Greek and Roman artifacts abound in the museum's extensive collection, which ranges from the well-known Parthenon sculptures to elaborate Roman jewelry and statues.
- Artifacts like the Portland Vase and the enormous monument of Amenhotep III bring the Classical world to life and provide us a concrete link to the creative and intellectual accomplishments of these ancient societies.

5. Asian Art and the Ming Treasure Ship:

- The work on display at the Asian galleries is varied and comes from China, Japan, Korea, and Southeast Asia. The famous Hoa Hakananai'a statue from Easter Island and the exquisite details of Chinese ceramics are among the highlights.

- A model of a massive ship from the Ming Dynasty, the Ming Treasure Ship represents China's exploration and naval power in the fifteenth century.

Visiting Tips:

The vast collection of the British Museum might be intimidating, so schedule your visit carefully. Depending on your preferences, you may want to concentrate on particular galleries or themes.

Use the audio guides or guided tours offered by the museum to learn more in-depth information about the historical settings and important items.

The British Museum does not charge admission, although donations are accepted. To find out about events and special exhibitions, visit the museum's website.

For those interested in learning more about humanity's common past, the British Museum provides an insightful and mind-blowing experience with its enormous collection of artifacts from all cultures. It is a monument to the persistence of the search for knowledge and understanding as well as the connectivity of civilizations, serving as more than just a storehouse of relics.

Westminster Abbey: A Symbol of British Tradition

Westminster Abbey, an enduring symbol of British tradition and a masterpiece of Gothic architecture, stands resplendent in the heart of London. With a history dating back over a thousand years, this iconic abbey has witnessed coronations, royal weddings, and the final resting place of monarchs, poets, scientists, and statesmen, making it a living tapestry of British history and culture.

1. Architectural Grandeur:

- King Edgar established the initial abbey in the tenth century, and Henry III reconstructed it in the Gothic style in the thirteenth. The majestic façade embodies the spirit of medieval craftsmanship, with its elaborate stone carvings and flying buttresses.

- Soaring vaulted ceilings, stained glass windows, and elaborate stone tracery throughout the magnificent interior create an ambiance of spiritual devotion and majestic beauty.

2. Royal Coronations and Weddings:

- From William the Conqueror's coronation in 1066 to the present, Westminster Abbey has hosted every crowning. Several monarchs have been crowned in the Coronation Chair, a prominent location in the abbey.
- Many royal marriages have taken place in the abbey, including the union of Queen Elizabeth II and Prince Philip. Within the abbey is the Poets' Corner, which honors writers such as Charles Dickens and Geoffrey Chaucer.

3. Poets' Corner:

- Some of the finest literary geniuses in British history have their final resting place or memorial location at Poets' Corner, a literary monument within Westminster Abbey. Here, authors, poets, and dramatists including Robert Burns, Jane Austen, and William Shakespeare rest in eternal peace.
- Poets' Corner's calm atmosphere honors the lasting contributions these literary greats have made to Britain's cultural fabric.

4. The Lady Chapel and Henry VII's Chapel:

- Famous for its elaborate stained glass windows and magnificent fan-vaulted ceiling, the Lady Chapel is a magnificent example of English Perpendicular Gothic architecture.
- Westminster Abbey's Henry VII's Chapel is a magnificent example of Tudor building design. The richness of the Tudor era is reflected in the magnificent Tudor insignia that adorn the chapel and the finely carved fan vaulting.

5. The Grave of the Unknown Warrior:

- A moving monument is the Grave of the Unknown Warrior, which is located close to the west door. The King and other dignitaries

witnessed the 1920 burial of the nameless soldier, who served as a symbol for all those who died in World War I.
- The grave is a somber reminder of the many people who gave their lives in the service of their nation.

Visiting Tips:

Westminster Abbey is still a functioning church, so check the calendar for services. During the hours that are specified for visits, guests are invited.

If you would want to learn more about the background and significance of the different areas of the abbey, think about taking a guided tour.

It is forbidden to take pictures during services, so make appropriate plans before you go.

Westminster Abbey captures the spirit of British heritage with its regal beauty, centuries-old customs, and historical resonance. Inside its sacred walls, visitors are invited to participate in the rich tapestry of the country's history, serving as a tribute to the long-lasting linkages between the past, present, and future.

St. Paul's Cathedral: Architectural Splendor

With its magnificent dome and ageless elegance, St. Paul's Cathedral, a masterpiece of English Baroque architecture and a lasting emblem of London's skyline, graces the city. This famous cathedral, a source of spiritual inspiration and architectural wonder, has been the site of centuries' worth of historical events, such as royal festivities and national memorials. As such, it is a treasured landmark and a testament to Britain's rich cultural legacy.

1. Architectural Marvel:

- St. Paul's Cathedral, which was built by Sir Christopher Wren in the late 17th century following the Great Fire of London, is a magnificent example of English Baroque architecture. The famous dome, which pays homage to Wren's vision and skill, was modeled after the dome of St. Peter's Basilica in Rome.

- The façade of the cathedral, which is embellished with elaborate carvings and classical columns, exhibits a tasteful fusion of artistic detail with architectural accuracy.

2. Whispering Gallery and Dome Climb:

- Within the dome, the Whispering Gallery provides a singular auditory experience. Whispering is permitted along the outside of the gallery, and sound travels over the curved surface to provide conversation across a significant distance.
- For sweeping views of London, tourists with a spirit of adventure can climb even higher to the Stone Gallery and the Golden Gallery. Aside from offering an amazing view of the city, the ascent to the top of the dome offers an up-close look at the intricate architectural elements of the church.

3. The Nave and High Altar:

- Entering the nave of St. Paul's Cathedral reveals the cathedral's grandeur—a roomy and majestic area decorated with elaborate carvings and Corinthian columns. With its three aisles, the nave evokes awe and reverence.
- The center of attention for religious rites and festivities is the High Altar, which is housed beneath the famous dome. The American Memorial Chapel, the elaborate wrought-iron railings, and the mosaic floor all add to the visual richness of the cathedral.

4. The Crypt:

- There are many tombs and memorials in the crypt beneath St. Paul's Cathedral, one of which is that of Sir Christopher Wren. Notable people's tombs, including the Duke of Wellington and Admiral Lord Nelson, are situated here as well, adding to the crypt's prominence as a historical site for contemplation.

5. The Great Fire of London Monument:

- The Great Fire of London Monument, designed by Sir Christopher Wren and Dr. Robert Hooke, is a freestanding Doric column located near St. Paul's Cathedral. The monument commemorates the devastating fire that swept through London in 1666, and visitors can climb to the top for panoramic views of the city.

Visiting Tips:

For information on services and events, check the schedule. St. Paul's Cathedral is still an operational church. Attending concerts or taking part in services within the cathedral is recommended for visitors.

If you want to climb the dome's galleries, you'll need to get tickets in advance because space for this well-liked experience is limited.

To gain a comprehensive understanding of the cultural and architectural diversity of the area, take some time to explore the surrounding area, which includes the Millennium Bridge and Tate Modern.

With its magnificent dome and minute details, St. Paul's Cathedral is a living example of London's tenacity and cultural heritage, as well as a monument to Sir Christopher Wren's genius. Whether taking in the timeless beauty of its venerable architecture or feeling the peace within its hallowed walls, guests are welcome to enjoy this enduring emblem of London.

Chapter 3
Neighborhood Exploration

Soho: London's Entertainment Hub

Situated in the center of London's West End, Soho is a lively and diverse district that is a hive of innovation, culture, and entertainment. Soho, which is well-known for its vibrant ambiance, charming historic district, and wide range of attractions, enthralls both residents and tourists with its theaters, nightlife, culinary options, and vast array of artistic expression.

1. Theatrical Extravaganza:

- Soho offers a long theatrical tradition with a cluster of world-renowned theaters, including the Prince Edward Theatre, the Shaftesbury Theatre, and the London Palladium. These locations present a wide range of shows, from provocative plays to West End musicals, guaranteeing a theatrical spectacle to suit every taste.

2. Music and Nightlife:

- Soho's bustling nightlife is pulsating with the rhythm of the city. Iconic performances spanning jazz, rock, and blues have taken place at historic music venues like Ronnie Scott's Jazz Club and the 100 Club.
- Explore the unique array of bars, clubs, and pubs along the winding streets. These establishments provide a variety of experiences, from modern cocktail lounges to classic English pubs.

3. Culinary Delights:

- With food options for every taste, Soho is a culinary paradise. The food scene is as varied as the neighborhood itself, with Michelin-starred eateries and unique cafes both available.

- Berwick Street Market offers a taste of the area with its variety of street food vendors. The variety of dining options available in Soho, from conventional British fare to international cuisines, is indicative of the area's global impact.

4. Artistic Vibes:

- For a very long time, Soho has been a creative and artistic sanctuary. Discover the many art galleries in the region that feature cutting-edge exhibitions and modern artwork.
- Sitting next to Soho, Carnaby Street is a fashion and art lover's paradise. Vibrant street art fills the little streets, resulting in a dynamic and always changing urban canvas.

5. LGBTQ+ Heritage:

- With legendary locations like the Admiral Duncan and the Royal Vauxhall Tavern, Soho boasts a long LGBTQ+ heritage. The neighborhood is a friendly place that embraces diversity and holds festivals and activities all year long.
- In the center of Soho, Old Compton Street is a hub for LGBTQ+ activity and life. Due to its progressive and welcoming culture, the neighborhood has historically served as a haven for LGBTQ+ people.

Visiting Tips:

- Take a stroll through Soho to truly experience its vibrant atmosphere and find hidden treasures nestled in its winding lanes.
- For a taste of London's lively performing arts industry, check out a production at one of the famous theaters in Soho or attend a live performance.
- Discover Soho's nightlife by visiting a variety of hip bars and traditional pubs, each with a distinct vibe.

Soho, with its kaleidoscope of entertainment, pulsating energy, and cultural diversity, encapsulates the essence of London's dynamic spirit. Whether immersing yourself in the theater, savoring diverse cuisines, or reveling in the nightlife, Soho beckons as a captivating destination where the city's heartbeat resonates with artistic fervor and a celebration of life.

Notting Hill: Quaint Streets and Colorful Markets

Notting Hill is a quaint neighborhood in West London that is well-known for its busy markets, gorgeous streets, and distinct posh and bohemian attitudes. This neighborhood entices travelers with its quirky boutiques, diverse culinary scene, and rich cultural tapestry that reflects both tradition and modernity, even beyond the notoriety gained by the film of the same name and its colorful mansions.

1. Colorful Streets and Iconic Houses:

- Notting Hill is known with its rows of pastel-colored houses, creating an attractive and Instagram-worthy setting. Wander around neighborhoods like Westbourne Grove and Portobello Road and take in the colorful façade that have come to symbolize the neighborhood's uniqueness.
- The photo-worthy "Notting Hill" blue door is a well-known landmark and a lovely reminder of the neighborhood's appeal in motion pictures.

2. Portobello Road Market:

- Portobello Road Market, one of London's most famous markets, is a kaleidoscope of antiques, vintage fashion, and eclectic treasures. The market comes alive with street performers, lively vendors, and a lively atmosphere on weekends.
- Explore the market's diverse stalls, ranging from antique shops and vintage boutiques to artisanal food stalls, offering a sensory feast for shoppers and food enthusiasts alike.

3. Arts and Culture:

- Notting Hill has a thriving arts scene, with numerous galleries and independent art spaces. The Museum of Brands, Packaging, and Advertising is a nostalgic journey through consumer culture,

while The Gate Theatre offers cutting-edge performances in an intimate setting.
- The Electric Cinema, one of the oldest working cinemas in the country, adds a touch of vintage glamour to the neighborhood. Enjoy a film in plush leather seats with a side of gourmet snacks.

4. Culinary Delights:

- Notting Hill is a restaurant lover's paradise with a wide variety of restaurants. The neighborhood offers something for every taste, from Michelin-starred restaurants to charming cafes offering specialty coffee.
- A few of the restaurants that highlight the neighborhood's culinary diversity are The Ledbury, Ottolenghi, and Electric Diner.

5. Notting Hill Carnival:

- Notting Hill Carnival, an annual celebration of Caribbean culture, transforms the streets into a vibrant and rhythmic extravaganza. Held in August, the carnival features colorful parades, live music, and delicious Caribbean cuisine.
- Join the festivities to experience the lively spirit of the carnival, where the streets come alive with the infectious beats of calypso and reggae.

Visiting Tips:

- Visit Portobello Road Market on weekends for the full experience, but be prepared for crowds.
- Explore the lesser-known streets and mews for a quieter and more intimate view of Notting Hill's charm.
- Check for events and festivals happening in the area, as Notting Hill often hosts cultural and community celebrations.

Notting Hill, with its quaint streets and lively markets, captivates visitors with a harmonious blend of history, culture, and contemporary flair. Whether meandering through colorful streets, discovering unique treasures at the market, or savoring diverse flavors, Notting Hill invites you to immerse yourself in its distinctive and delightful atmosphere.

Camden Town: Alternative Culture and Markets

North London's Camden Town is a vibrant, eclectic neighborhood that is home to a wide variety of markets, vibrant street art, and alternative culture. Renowned for its eclectic ambiance and flourishing music scene, Camden enthralls tourists with its recognizable markets, one-of-a-kind stores, and an inventive spirit that defines its unique identity.

1. Camden Market:

    - The hub of Camden Town is the vast network of markets known as Camden Market. It offers a treasure trove of unique things and is divided into numerous areas, such as the Stables Market, Camden Lock Market, and Inverness Street Market.
    - For those looking for unusual and unusual items, Camden Market is a treasure trove, offering everything from handcrafted crafts and antique clothing to foreign food and odd souvenirs.

2. Street Art and Alternative Culture:

    - The streets of Camden are adorned with vibrant and thought-provoking street art. Wander through the Camden Market area to discover murals, graffiti, and installations that reflect the alternative and rebellious spirit of the neighborhood.

- The Electric Ballroom, a historic music venue, embodies Camden's alternative culture, hosting live music events, club nights, and eclectic performances.

3. The Camden Locks:

- Camden is traversed by the Regent's Canal, and the locks provide a beautiful backdrop. Take a leisurely stroll down the canal, see the boats as they pass through the locks, and take in the laid-back atmosphere.
- Look around the restaurants and cafés along the water to find a beautiful place to eat or have some drinks.

4. Music Scene and Live Venues:

- Camden Town has been a crucible for emerging musical talent for decades. Iconic venues like The Roundhouse, The Dublin Castle, and KOKO have hosted legendary performances by artists ranging from The Rolling Stones to Amy Winehouse.
- Experience Camden's live music scene by checking out the diverse range of gigs happening at various venues throughout the neighborhood.

5. Camden Market After Dark:

- Camden Market After Dark is when the market has a new atmosphere in the evening. The market stays open late, resulting in a distinctive setting that includes food vendors, live music, and a more laid-back vibe.
- Investigate the market after dark to witness its metamorphosis into a vibrant, animated center of artistic expression.

Visiting Tips:

Weekends can get busy, so if you want a more leisurely shopping experience, visit Camden Market during the week.

Discover hidden jewels, old stores, and smaller markets by exploring the alleyways and backstreets.

Accept Camden's varied food culture, which offers street cuisine from all around the world and flavors from around the globe.

For those looking to escape the norm, Camden Town entices them with its colorful street life, unique markets, and alternative culture. Camden welcomes you to embrace its distinct and rebellious attitude, whether you choose to embrace its unique and rebellious spirit by just taking in the music-filled environment, exploring its nooks and crannies, or immersing yourself in the creative energy of the markets.

Shoreditch: Trendy Art and Street Food Scene

East London's Shoreditch is a gritty, hip district known for its cutting-edge art, energetic street culture, and developing street food scene. Known for its inventive galleries, unique street art, and wide range of gastronomic pleasures, Shoreditch enthralls tourists with its creative energy and fusion of modern and historic influences.

1. Street Art Galleries:

- With its vibrant and provocative street art, Shoreditch is a canvas of urban expression. Many street art galleries can be found in the area, such as the well-known Shoreditch Art Wall and the Nomadic Community Gardens, where street artists are free to display their artistic abilities.
- Take a street art walking tour to learn more about the histories behind the murals and the dynamic environment of this outdoor gallery.

2. Brick Lane:

- The vibrant Shoreditch street Brick Lane is a mingling pot of cuisines, styles, and civilizations. Stroll down the street and explore the unique markets, local boutiques, and vintage stores.
- One of Brick Lane's best features is its varied culinary scene, which includes everything from classic English breakfasts to curry joints and artisanal bakeries.

3. Shoreditch High Street:

- Shoreditch High Street is a hub of creativity and business. Discover the newest trends in fashion, art, and design in the area's pop-up shops, designer boutiques, and independent shops.
- Built out of shipping containers, The Boxpark Shoreditch offers a lively ambiance, a range of independent stores, and dining options.

4. Shoreditch Art Wall:

- One of the most recognizable sights in the area is the Shoreditch Art Wall, a dynamic canvas used by street painters. The expansive mural area adds to the vibrant and ephemeral art environment in the neighborhood by showcasing the works of both local and foreign artists.
- For people strolling around the streets, the Shoreditch Art Wall's vivid colors and minute details provide a visual feast.

5. Street Food Markets:

- The street food scene in Shoreditch is flourishing, with markets such as Dinerama and Pump Street Market providing a wide variety of mouthwatering options. These markets provide everything for every taste, from international street cuisine to handcrafted pizzas and gourmet burgers.
- These vibrant street food markets offer a lively atmosphere, an array of distinct flavors, and the communal spirit of dining al fresco.

Visiting Tips:

Take a stroll through Shoreditch to see the bustling street life and find hidden treasures nestled in the alleyways.

Weekends might get crowded, so for a more laid-back experience, visit the street art locations during the weekdays.

For information on pop-up markets, exhibitions, and street performances in Shoreditch, check out the events calendar.

For those looking for the latest in modern culture, Shoreditch is a vibrant playground with its unique fusion of fashion, art, and culinary innovation. Shoreditch welcomes you to embrace its trendsetting energy and experience the ever-evolving creativity of East London, whether you're soaking in the bright street art, browsing independent stores, or indulging in the variety of street food offers.

Greenwich: Maritime History and Greenwich Mean Time

Greenwich, a historic and picturesque district in southeast London, is renowned for its maritime legacy, royal connections, and its pivotal role in defining time. Steeped in history and offering a serene riverside setting, Greenwich invites visitors to explore its maritime heritage, iconic landmarks, and lush green spaces.

1. Maritime Greenwich:

- Maritime Greenwich, a UNESCO World Heritage Site that includes well-known landmarks, has a long maritime history. The region's naval past is reflected in the architectural marvel Queen's House and the Old Royal Naval College, both of which were created by Sir Christopher Wren.
- Explore the world of 19th-century maritime trade with an interactive adventure aboard the Cutty Sark, a historic tea clipper turned museum. Explore the decks of the ship and discover more about its global travels.

2. Royal Observatory and Greenwich Mean Time (GMT):

- The world's time is measured at the Royal Observatory, which is situated on a hill in Greenwich Park. The observatory is situated at the intersection of the Prime Meridian Line, which indicates 0 degrees longitude. This allows visitors to stand simultaneously in the eastern and western hemispheres.
- Visit the museum at the Royal Observatory to learn about the evolution of the Greenwich Mean Time (GMT) and the history of

timekeeping. Every day at 1 p.m., the famous red time ball atop Flamsteed House descends, following a 19th-century custom.

3. Greenwich Park:

- A huge and exquisitely manicured royal park, Greenwich Park provides breathtaking views of the city skyline and the River Thames. With its old trees, flower beds, and strolling routes, the park offers a tranquil haven.
- Ascend the hill to get a bird's-eye perspective over London, highlighting famous sites like the Shard and St. Paul's Cathedral in the distance.

4. National Maritime Museum:

- The largest marine museum in the world is called the National Maritime Museum, and it is situated in Greenwich. Discover a large array of nautical memorabilia, ship models, and navigational aids that provide insights into the history of British naval forces.
- The exhibitions of the museum span a broad spectrum of subjects, including naval combat, exploration, navigation, and the influence of the sea on cultures worldwide.

5. The Royal Borough of Greenwich:

- As a recognized Royal Borough, Greenwich boasts quaint streets with boutique stores, quaint bars, and historic buildings along them. Explore the market at Greenwich Market, which features delectable street cuisine, arts and crafts, and antiques.
- The Old Royal Naval College is a must-see site that perfectly embodies Greenwich's royal and maritime ties with its opulent architecture, riverbank location, and cultural events.

Visiting Tips:

To escape the weekend crowds, especially around renowned attractions like the Royal Observatory, schedule your vacation to Greenwich during the week.

For a picturesque and leisurely introduction to the area, combine a trip to Greenwich with a leisurely boat ride along the River Thames.

See what's happening at the National Maritime Museum and the Old Royal Naval College; both places frequently have performances and cultural displays.

With its maritime charm, historical royal sites, and contributions to timekeeping, Greenwich entices tourists to travel back in time and discover the intricate web of British naval and astrological history. Greenwich, on the banks of the River Thames, offers a beautiful blend of antiquity and tranquillity, whether you're standing on the Prime Meridian Line or strolling through the elegant park.

Chapter 4
Parks and Outdoor Activities

Hyde Park: Serenity in the Heart of London

A vast green space in the center of London, Hyde Park represents peace amid the busy metropolis. Hyde Park is a refuge of natural beauty and leisure delight that draws both locals and tourists to escape the bustle of the city with its verdant surroundings, placid lakes, and well-known attractions.

1. Serpentine Lake and Boating:

   - Located in the center of Hyde Park, Serpentine Lake is a sizable recreational body of water that provides a lovely backdrop for leisurely walks and boat rides. Hire a rowboat or pedalboat to float on the calm waterways and see the park's surrounds from a different angle.

2. Kensington Gardens:

   - Kensington Gardens and Hyde Park blend together to create a vast green space. Kensington Gardens offers a calm setting for reflection and leisure thanks to its tasteful flowerbeds, majestic statues, and charming Italian Gardens.

3. The Serpentine Galleries:

   - Situated on the periphery of Serpentine Lake, the Serpentine Galleries present modern artwork within a serene environment. The Serpentine Pavilion, an annual architectural commission, lends an element of originality and imagination to the park's scenery.

4. Speakers' Corner:

- Speakers' Corner, a historic free-speech zone, allowing anyone to share their ideas on many topics in a public forum. The custom, which originated in the middle of the 1800s, is still a lively forum for discussion and debate.

5. Kensington Palace:

- Situated on the western boundary of Hyde Park, Kensington Palace is a historically significant royal palace. Take in the stunning gardens that encircle the palace and discover more about the lives of illustrious former occupants such as Princess Diana and Queen Victoria.

6. The Diana, Princess of Wales Memorial Fountain:

- Located in Hyde Park, the Diana, Princess of Wales Memorial Fountain is a tranquil circular water feature honoring Princess Diana. Because of the design, guests can wade in the chilly waters, fostering an area for reflection and contemplation.

7. The Hyde Park Corner:

- The Hyde Park Corner, a historic gateway at the southeast corner of the park, is marked by the Wellington Arch. Ascend the arch for panoramic views of the surrounding area, including Buckingham Palace and the bustling streets of London.

Visiting Tips:

Savor refreshments at one of the park's cafes or have a leisurely picnic on the vast lawns.

See the calendar for upcoming concerts and seasonal activities in Hyde Park, including as outdoor music festivals and cultural events.

Take a leisurely stroll along the trails surrounded by trees or rent a bicycle to explore the park's expansive grounds.

Hyde Park is a peaceful haven in the middle of London where people can relax, reconnect with nature, and find comfort in a beautiful blend of natural beauty and historic relics. Whether you're looking for a quiet getaway or something to do with the family, Hyde Park is a beloved urban haven that offers a timeless diversion from the hectic pace of the city.

Regent's Park: A Haven for Nature Lovers

Regent's Park, a verdant gem nestled in the heart of London, stands as a haven for nature lovers and a testament to the city's commitment to green spaces. With its meticulously landscaped gardens, tranquil lakes, and a diverse array of recreational activities, Regent's Park invites visitors to escape the urban bustle and immerse themselves in the beauty of nature.

1. The Regent's Park Gardens:

- The park is well known for its exquisite gardens, each having a distinct personality. With its colorful rose beds and amazing collection of more than 12,000 roses, Queen Mary's Gardens offers a fragrant and visually striking setting.
- The Avenue Gardens provides a calm setting for leisurely strolls and picnics. It has a traditional plan with beautiful seasonal exhibits.

2. Boating on the Regent's Park Lake:

- There is a calm lake in the park where guests can take leisurely boat excursions. Hire a rowboat or pedalboat to explore the calm waters and take in the beautiful surroundings, which include the lake's recognizable duck population.

3. The Open Air Theatre:

- Regent's Park Open Air Theatre, a unique cultural centre in the heart of the park, presents outdoor performances throughout the summer. See a play or musical outside in the open air, among a plethora of verdant foliage.
-

4. Primrose Hill:

- Adjacent to Regent's Park, Primrose Hill provides a panoramic view of the London skyline. A gentle ascent to the summit rewards visitors with breathtaking vistas, making it an ideal spot for sunrise or sunset gatherings.

5. ZSL London Zoo:

- Regent's Park is a great place for animal lovers to visit because it is home to the renowned ZSL London Zoo. Discover the fascinating voyage through the animal kingdom by perusing the zoo's varied exhibits, which include the Gorilla Kingdom and the Land of the Lions.

6. The Inner Circle and Sports Facilities:

- The tree-lined Inner Circle is a peaceful route for jogging and walking. Nearby sports facilities, such as tennis courts and the Regent's Park Hub for cyclists, serve guests who are active.

7. The Regent's Canal:

- The Regent's Canal borders the northern edge of the park, providing a scenic waterside promenade. Stroll along the canal towpath, observe passing canal boats, and experience a serene escape amidst the urban landscape.

Visiting Tips:

Come to Queen Mary's Gardens at different times of the year to see the blossoms and the gardens' shifting hues.

For a more thorough experience, think about combining your visit to Regent's Park with visits to neighboring sites like the London Zoo or Camden Market.

For information about upcoming special events, such as park-based outdoor concerts and cultural festivals, check the schedule.

Regent's Park welcomes nature enthusiasts to relax, explore, and enjoy the various aspects of the natural world right in the middle of London with its tasteful blend of carefully planned landscapes and recreational amenities. Regent's Park is a tribute to the city's dedication to maintaining green areas for the enjoyment of both locals and visitors, whether taking in the beauty of the gardens or engaging in outdoor activities.

Hampstead Heath: Stunning Views and Open Spaces

Hampstead Heath, a sprawling expanse of natural beauty in the north of London, is a haven for those seeking stunning views, open spaces, and a respite from urban life. With its rolling meadows, ancient woodlands, and panoramic vantage points, Hampstead Heath offers a tranquil escape that captivates nature enthusiasts and strollers alike.

1. Parliament Hill:

- One of London's highest peaks, Parliament Hill offers an unparalleled overview of the city. Views of the vast skyline, which includes famous sites like St. Paul's Cathedral, the Shard, and the London Eye, are breathtaking as guests climb the hill. This well-liked location is ideal for strolls, picnics, or just relaxing while taking in the metropolis.

2. Hampstead Ponds:

- The Mixed Bathing Pond, the Kenwood Ladies' Pond, and the Highgate Men's Pond make up the Hampstead Ponds, which provide a delightful and unusual outdoor swimming experience. These ponds, which are surrounded by Hampstead Heath's breathtaking scenery, offer a peaceful haven for anyone seeking a quiet place to cool off.

3. Kenwood House:

- Nestled amidst exquisitely designed grounds is Kenwood House, a magnificent neoclassical home from the 18th century. Renowned artists like Rembrandt and Vermeer are among the outstanding artworks in the estate's collection. Explore the opulence of the mansion, take in art exhibits, and relax in the serene environs of the immaculately kept grounds.

4. Ancient Woodlands:

- The historic woodlands of Hampstead Heath, such as the West Meadow and the Vale of Health, envelop visitors in a peaceful, natural world. An immersive experience in nature is offered by winding roads that wind through deep forest. These woodlands are ideal for peaceful reflection, birdwatching, and discovering the variety of plants that make up this protected area.

5. The Hill Garden and Pergola:

- A hidden gem in Hampstead Heath, the Hill Garden and Pergola boasts exquisitely designed gardens filled with flowers and climbing vines. Visitors can enjoy a gorgeous location and breathtaking views of the surrounding flora from the big Edwardian pergola. Taking a leisurely stroll in this charming garden is a lovely way to unwind.

6. Hampstead Heath Extension:

- The Heath Extension adds more open spaces, sports fields, and woodland pathways to the vastness of Hampstead Heath. This enlargement gives guests the chance to go on longer excursions and explorations and fully immerse themselves in the natural splendor that characterizes this large park.

7. Golders Hill Park:

- Situated inside the boundaries of Hampstead Heath, Golders Hill Park is a complex attraction. With its attractive water garden, ornamental gardens, and small zoo, this park is a great place for families to spend time together. Discover a variety of animal species, take in the calm of the well-kept grounds, and enjoy the Butterfly House.

Visiting Tips:

A network of trails and paths allows you to explore the enormous area of Hampstead Heath, therefore it's best to have a map with you for easy navigation.

Go at different times of the year to get the most out of the experience. See the evolution of the Heath as the spring gives flowers, the autumn offers changing leaves, and the winter brings peaceful calm.

Bring a picnic to eat on one of the Heath's wide meadows; it's the ideal way to unwind and take in the beauty of nature.

With its variety of landscapes, cultural assets, and recreational opportunities, Hampstead Heath is a prime example of London's dedication to protecting green spaces for the enjoyment and wellbeing of both locals and tourists. In the midst of the city, Hampstead Heath provides a revitalizing haven for those seeking stunning views, discovering historic woodlands, or just relaxing in the gardens.

Kensington Gardens: Greenery by the Palaces

Tucked away in the center of London, Kensington Gardens is a veritable tapestry of greenery that melds perfectly with the stately architecture of old palaces. Once Kensington Palace's private grounds, this vast green refuge is now calm and peaceful, inviting tourists to explore its beautiful scenery and cultural treasures.

The Serpentine Lake: Kensington Gardens embraces the tranquility of the Serpentine Lake, a sprawling water expanse that mirrors the lush green surroundings. Its shores provide a retreat for leisurely walks, while the water itself offers a canvas for the gentle strokes of rowboats, creating a symphony of nature and recreation.

Kensington Palace: At the heart of the gardens stands Kensington Palace, an architectural marvel with a storied past. Its regal corridors echo with the whispers of history, having housed royalty through the ages. The Sunken Garden, a hidden gem within the palace grounds, adds a touch of elegance with its vibrant blooms and serene ambiance.

Italian Gardens: A tribute to classical aesthetics, the Italian Gardens captivate with their symmetrical allure. Fountains dance amidst meticulously manicured flowerbeds, and sculptures adorn this oasis, evoking the spirit of Renaissance opulence. A sensory feast unfolds as visitors wander through this beautifully designed retreat.

The Albert Memorial: Southwards, the gardens open up to the grandeur of the Albert Memorial, a tribute to Prince Albert's legacy. Amidst ornate sculptures and intricate mosaics, this monument stands as a testament to timeless love and artistic excellence, inviting contemplation in its majestic shadow.

The Peter Pan Statue: A whimsical encounter awaits those who venture westward, where the mischievous spirit of Peter Pan is immortalized in bronze. The statue captures the essence of J.M. Barrie's enchanting tale, inviting onlookers to join the eternal adventure of eternal youth.

The Diana, Princess of Wales Memorial Playground: A celebration of childhood joy, the Memorial Playground is a vibrant space inspired by the whimsy of Peter Pan. Children explore a pirate ship, traverse a sensory trail, and engage in boundless play, all within the embrace of this playful sanctuary.

The Long Water: Parallel to Kensington Palace, the Long Water offers a tranquil stretch along tree-lined banks. The pathways along its shores provide a quiet escape, allowing contemplative strolls amidst the natural beauty that frames this historic landscape.

Visiting Tips: Combine history with leisure by complementing a stroll through the gardens with an exploration of the regal interiors of Kensington Palace. Indulge in a leisurely picnic, savoring the ambiance and green expanses that make Kensington Gardens an urban retreat. Experience the gardens' transformative charm by visiting during different seasons, each unveiling a distinct facet of nature's allure.

Kensington Gardens, where verdant landscapes meet regal splendor, beckon explorers to wander through its timeless beauty, inviting an immersive encounter with nature and history in the heart of London.

Thames Path: Riverside Walks and Iconic Views

The Thames Path unfolds as a captivating journey along the riverbanks, offering a rich tapestry of riverside walks and iconic views that encapsulate the essence of London's past and present.

1. **Tower Bridge to London Bridge:** The journey begins in the shadow of Tower Bridge, an iconic symbol of London's architectural prowess. Strolling along the South Bank toward London Bridge, the bustling riverside promenade becomes a sensory delight, with street performers, markets, and a panorama of historical landmarks setting the stage for an immersive experience.
2. **Tate Modern and Millennium Bridge:** Approaching the Tate Modern, a former power station transformed into a contemporary art haven, the Thames Path unveils the sleek Millennium Bridge. This modern suspension bridge provides unparalleled views of St. Paul's Cathedral, creating a harmonious blend of historic and contemporary London.
3. **Shakespeare's Globe Theatre and The Golden Hinde:** Continuing the journey, the path meanders past the faithful reconstruction of Shakespeare's Globe Theatre, a homage to the Bard's enduring legacy. Nearby, The Golden Hinde, a meticulous replica of Sir Francis Drake's historic ship, adds a maritime touch to the riverside, invoking tales of exploration and seafaring adventures.
4. **South Bank Centre and London Eye:** As the path unfolds, the South Bank Centre comes into view, with its cultural venues and the iconic London Eye dominating the skyline. The vibrant atmosphere along the riverside blends contemporary art, live performances, and stunning cityscape vistas. The London Eye, a colossal observation wheel, becomes a focal point, providing a unique perspective of the metropolis.
5. **Westminster and Houses of Parliament:** Approaching Westminster, the Thames Path reveals the grandeur of the Houses of Parliament and the timeless Big Ben. The riverside ambiance transforms as historic structures line the path, offering a poignant reflection on the interplay of politics and architecture. The

panoramic view across the river captures the essence of London's rich history.
6. **Embankment Gardens and Cleopatra's Needle:** Venturing onward, the path leads to the tranquility of the Embankment Gardens, adorned with lush greenery and intricate sculptures. Cleopatra's Needle, an ancient Egyptian obelisk flanked by sphinxes, adds a touch of exotic history to the riverside, symbolizing London's global connections.
7. **The Shard and Tower of London:** As the Thames Path approaches its conclusion, the modern silhouette of The Shard commands attention. This architectural marvel stands in contrast to the historical Tower of London nearby, creating a captivating juxtaposition of old and new. The convergence of these landmarks along the riverside walk serves as a powerful testament to London's enduring legacy.

Visiting Tips:

- Embrace spontaneity along the Thames Path, allowing for detours to riverside cafes, art installations, and hidden gems.
- Experience the magic of the river at sunset or evening, when the city lights illuminate iconic landmarks along the riverbanks.
- Consider complementing the walk with a leisurely boat ride or cruise along the Thames to gain a fresh perspective of London's landmarks.

The Thames Path, a winding journey along the river's edge, beckons adventurers to immerse themselves in the dynamic blend of London's history and contemporary vibrancy. From historic landmarks to modern architectural wonders, each step along this iconic walk reveals the city's character, unfolding a narrative shaped by the ever-flowing waters of the River Thames.

Chapter 5
Culinary Adventures

Traditional British Cuisine: Exploring Classics

Embarking on a culinary journey through traditional British cuisine unveils a rich tapestry of flavors, where time-honored classics hold a special place in the hearts and palates of locals. From hearty pies to delicate pastries, the exploration of these culinary gems provides a genuine taste of British gastronomic traditions.

1. **Sunday Roast:** A cherished custom, the Sunday roast unites families over a feast of roasted meats, Yorkshire pudding, crunchy roast potatoes, and a variety of seasonal vegetables. This traditional British dish is a hearty celebration of shared dining that is frequently consumed in family homes or pubs.
2. **Fish and Chips:** A trip through British food history would not be complete without sampling the classic Fish and Chips. Chunky golden fries are a delightful accompaniment to crispy battered fish, usually haddock or cod. This meal, which is typically wrapped in newspaper, is a reflection of the coastal culinary tradition.

3. **Full English Breakfast:** A filling start to the day, the Full English Breakfast comes with a substantial selection of bacon, sausages, eggs, baked beans, and black pudding. This hearty breakfast is a cultural staple that powers the day. It's typically served with toast and a strong tea cup.
4. **Beef Wellington:** A famous dish that elevates British pastry and culinary skill is beef Wellington. Layers of prosciutto and mushroom duxelles encircle a soft beef fillet, which is then coated in puff pastry and baked to golden perfection. This dish is a perfect example of British cooking flair.
5. **Cornish Pasty:** Originating in Cornwall, the Cornish Pasty is a savory pastry stuffed with a substantial blend of meat, potatoes, and veggies. Originally designed as a quick lunch for miners, this portable treat has grown to be a beloved snack throughout the nation.
6. **Afternoon Tea:** Afternoon Tea, a refined tradition, invites indulgence in delicate sandwiches, scones with clotted cream and jam, and an assortment of pastries. Paired with a pot of tea, this elegant ritual celebrates the art of leisure and socializing.
7. **Shepherd's Pie:** Shepherd's Pie is a comforting dish that epitomizes British home cooking. Ground lamb or beef, cooked with vegetables and savory gravy, is crowned with a layer of creamy mashed potatoes and baked until golden. This wholesome meal exudes warmth and familiarity.

Visiting Tips:

Visit neighborhood pubs for a genuine taste of British staples; the atmosphere there improves the dining experience.

Take part in customary gatherings or celebrations that highlight local specialties and offer a glimpse into the varied gastronomic scene.

Accept the custom of tea time and try a range of teas to go with savory and sweet snacks.

A delicious trip through time is revealed when one investigates traditional British cuisine; each dish narrates a tale of comfort, tradition, and culinary artistry. Sunday Roasts and Afternoon Tea, with their conviviality and sophisticated refinement, are cultural icons that continue to define the depth of British cuisine.

Multicultural London: Global Flavors

Delving into the multicultural tapestry of London is an exploration of global flavors that have found a home in this vibrant metropolis. The city's diverse communities have woven a culinary mosaic that reflects the richness of cultures from around the world, inviting locals and visitors alike to embark on a gastronomic journey.

1. **Brick Lane:** Located in the center of East London, Brick Lane is a cultural melting pot that is especially well-known for its thriving Bangladeshi community. The air is filled with the heady smells of curry houses, drawing people in with the prospect of mouthwatering food. Brick Lane is a must-visit location for anybody looking to sample South Asian cuisine, offering everything from inventive fusion dishes to classic curries.
2. **Chinatown:** London's Chinatown, nestled in the heart of the West End, beckons with its lively atmosphere and a plethora of authentic Asian eateries. Here, one can savor traditional dim sum, Peking duck, and a myriad of regional Chinese specialties. The vibrant red lanterns and bustling streets create an immersive experience reminiscent of East Asia.
3. **Little Italy in Soho:** Soho's Frith Street is home to London's Little Italy, where Italian flavors flourish. Cozy trattorias and gelaterias line the streets, serving up classic pasta dishes, thin-crust pizzas, and delectable gelato. The atmosphere exudes the warmth of Italian hospitality, making it a culinary haven for lovers of Mediterranean cuisine.
4. **Edgware Road:** Edgware Road, known for its Middle Eastern influence, boasts a diverse array of Lebanese, Syrian, and Persian eateries. The tantalizing aromas of shawarma, falafel, and kebabs fill the air, creating a sensory journey through the vibrant and flavorful world of Middle Eastern cuisine.
5. **Brixton Market:** Brixton Market, located in South London, reflects the Afro-Caribbean influence that has shaped the culinary landscape of the area. The market's stalls and eateries offer a delightful array of jerk chicken, roti, and other Caribbean

specialties. This cultural hub celebrates the diversity of flavors from the Caribbean diaspora.

6. **Borough Market:** Borough Market, near London Bridge, is a gastronomic paradise that brings together global flavors under one roof. From French cheeses to Spanish paella, Turkish delights to Ethiopian injera, the market is a celebration of culinary diversity. It is a testament to London's role as a global culinary crossroads.

7. **Southall:** Southall, often referred to as "Little India," is a haven for lovers of Indian cuisine. The vibrant streets are lined with sari shops and spice markets, and the air is infused with the aromas of curry and spices. From traditional dosas to mouthwatering curries, Southall offers an authentic taste of India in the heart of London.

Visiting Tips:

Examine culinary festivals and cultural gatherings that highlight the wide range of culinary options available in London.

Interact with locals to find genuine restaurants and hidden treasures that aren't always well-known.

Seize the chance to sample inventive fusion cuisine that combines the greatest ingredients from many different cooking traditions.

With its international flavors, multicultural London offers a gastronomic journey where each neighborhood's restaurants tell a different tale. The culinary scene in the city is a reflection of the diversity and connection of its multicultural population, from the spices of Brick Lane to the dim sum of Chinatown.

Borough Market: A Gastronomic Paradise

Tucked down under the ancient arches next to London Bridge, Borough Market has long been a gastronomic haven, drawing both locals and tourists into its colorful embrace. This culinary utopia emerges beyond the daily grind, providing a sensory voyage through an enthralling tapestry of international flavors and artisanal craftsmanship.

1. **A Tapestry of Flavors:** Entering Borough Market fills the air with the tantalizing aromas of many different cuisines. With roots in the twelfth century, the market has developed into a thriving festival of fine food. Wander along its bustling avenues, where devoted artisans present their wares, transforming the market into an enthralling exhibition of tastes.
2. **Artisanal Delights:** The artisanal goods of Borough Market are its main attraction. Enter a world of handcrafted treats where bakers exhibit freshly baked bread, chocolatiers entice with exquisite confections, and cheese mongers proudly display their wheels of artisan cheese. Every taste is a tribute to the artisan's passion, as each stand shares a tale of commitment and skill.
3. **Culinary Diversity:** The allure of Borough Market is its capacity to take your taste senses on a culinary journey across countries. Explore the varied kiosks in the market to find French crepes skillfully flipped before your eyes, Turkish mezze arranged in vibrant arrays, Ethiopian injera waiting to be devoured, and Spanish paella cooking in big pots. The delight of discovering

such a diverse array of international cuisines is enhanced by the market's outdoor atmosphere.
4. **Farm-Fresh Produce:** Seasonally-various flavors and a rainbow of hues are showcased by local farmers as they proudly present their produce. Because of Borough Market's dedication to providing farm-fresh goods, you can be guaranteed to experience the genuine spirit of regional agriculture. The market stalls were brimming with the abundance of the harvest, from colorful fruits to crunchy veggies.
5. **Gourmet Street Food:** For those looking for new gastronomic experiences, Borough Market is a sanctuary for street food connoisseurs. An alluring ambiance is created by the tantalizing aroma of sizzling pans, the cracking of grills, and the buzz of food connoisseurs. Savor a handcrafted sausage roll, indulge in a juicy burger, or discover unique street food options from across the world.
6. **Culinary Events and Workshops:** Borough Market is a thriving location for both professionals and food fans, beyond its busy stalls. Numerous events are held in the market, such as tasting sessions guided by seasoned food specialists and cooking demonstrations by well-known chefs. Interact with the food community to learn about the creativity that goes into creating your favorite dishes and maybe even discover a new favorite flavor.
7. **Sustainability and Ethical Sourcing:** In addition to being a sensory extravaganza, Borough Market promotes ethical sourcing and sustainability. Numerous suppliers gladly follow environmentally friendly procedures, demonstrating a dedication to conscientious consumption. There's more to appreciate than just the delicious food when you realize that your gastronomic adventure is in line with environmental concern.

Visiting Tips:

If you want to experience Borough Market to the fullest, get there early to beat the crowds and take your time browsing the stalls.

Talk to the enthusiastic vendors; their tales provide a deeper understanding to the goods they sell.

To learn more about the various products and culinary traditions, peruse the market's active roster of special events, tastings, and workshops.

With its long history and dedication to fine dining, Borough Market is more than simply a market—a it's symbol of London's unwavering passion for cuisine. Each visit turns into a celebration of the city's lively food scene's diversity and energy, as well as flavors and master craftsmanship. The past and present come together in Borough Market to create an immersive experience that goes beyond simple consumption to become a rich and social celebration of food.

Afternoon Tea: A British Tradition

A beloved custom that has stood the test of time, afternoon tea is central to British society. This delicious culinary experience is the essence of refinement, elegance, and conviviality, having evolved from its aristocratic beginnings to become a beloved ritual for both locals and tourists. Being seated at the afternoon tea table is an immersive experience immersed in the elegance and sophistication of British teatime, not merely a meal.

1. **Origins of Afternoon Tea:** Many people attribute the invention of afternoon tea to Anna, the Duchess of Bedford, who lived in the early 1800s. She proposed the notion of a mid-afternoon meal consisting of tea, sandwiches, and desserts because she was used to the extended interval between lunch and supper. This tasteful resolution quickly became well-known and became a phenomenon in culture.
2. **The Classic Components:** Three primary ingredients make up a typical afternoon tea, and each is carefully prepared to produce a pleasing harmony of flavors. The base was laid with delicate finger sandwiches filled with egg salad, smoked salmon, and cucumber. After that, warm scones with strawberry jam and clotted cream take center stage. A variety of cakes, pastries, and other sweet delights are served at the end to demonstrate the pastry chef's culinary skills.
3. **The Art of Brewing:** Afternoon tea's main ingredient, tea, is an art form in and of itself. There is a wide variety of teas available, from traditional Earl Grey to unique combinations. The art of

brewing tea is a meticulous process that guarantees a fragrant and tasty cup every time. The act of pouring and drinking brings a calm element to the scene as a whole.

4. **The Setting:** Afternoon tea is an experience shaped by its surroundings rather than just a meal. The ideal setting for this sophisticated event includes beautiful restaurants, historic hotels, and traditional tearooms. A sophisticated yet laid-back ambiance is created by the use of beautiful china, immaculate linen, and live piano music on the table.
5. **Modern Variations:** Even while afternoon tea's fundamentals are still based on history, contemporary iterations have evolved to suit a range of palates. Some places serve themed teas with creative flavor combinations and modern touches. There are also options for vegans, gluten-free people, and others following particular diets, making Afternoon Tea a treat that is enjoyed by all.
6. **Afternoon Tea Etiquette:** Afternoon tea has its own set of customs and protocol for guests. Sandwiches should be consumed first, then scones and desserts; this order helps you enjoy the flavors in a planned way. The subtleties of holding a teacup elegantly and engaging in courteous conversation add to the whole experience and atmosphere.
7. **Celebratory Occasions:** Afternoon Tea is used to commemorate special occasions in addition to being a regular indulgence. Birthdays, anniversaries, and bridal showers are frequently held in the refined setting of a tea shop, where the happy sound of teacup clinking creates a melodious celebration.

Visiting Tips:

To guarantee a desired place for your Afternoon Tea experience, reservations are advised, particularly at well-known tea businesses.

Wearing elegant yet laid-back clothing heightens the feeling of occasion and improves the whole experience.

Discovering the many regional varieties of Afternoon Tea in the UK is a lovely opportunity to experience new tastes and culinary customs.

Beyond just a culinary treat, afternoon tea is a celebration of enduring customs, sophisticated tastes, and the art of sociability. Indulging in the traditional elements or going for the modern twists, taking part in this distinctly British custom provides a moment of calm and a hint of sophistication in the middle of our hectic life. Not only is afternoon tea a meal, but it's also an opportunity to appreciate the elegance of custom and the skill of food preparation.

Michelin-Starred Dining: Fine Culinary Experiences

A Michelin-starred restaurant is the height of culinary perfection; every dish is a work of art, and the whole dining experience is transformed into an artistic endeavor. The esteemed Michelin Guide, which has its roots in France, has come to represent culinary refinement and leads discriminating customers to restaurants that push the envelope in terms of flavor, originality, and friendliness. Embracing a Michelin-starred culinary adventure is more than simply a meal; it's an exploration of a world where creativity, accuracy, and passion come together to create unique dining experiences.

1. **The Michelin Star Prestige:** The coveted stars in the Michelin Guide are a symbol of culinary distinction given to restaurants that serve food of the highest caliber. Restaurants can be awarded one, two, or three stars, which represent different levels of excellence. Every star indicates a chef's commitment to excellence and guarantees an amazing dining experience.
2. **Culinary Innovation and Creativity:** Dining with a Michelin star elevates the standard and displays culinary ingenuity and inventiveness. Prominent chefs elevate each dish to a sensory masterpiece by pushing the limits of flavor, texture, and presentation. The ingredients serve as a creative palette that both surprises and delights the palate, while the menu acts as a canvas.
3. **Impeccable Service and Hospitality:** The eating experience at restaurants with Michelin stars goes beyond the food. A flawless execution of the dinner is dependent on the presence of impeccable service and hospitality. Diners are immersed in a world where attention to detail is crucial, from the friendly greeting at the door to the expert direction of the sommeliers.

4. **Seasonal and Locally Sourced Ingredients:** The focus on locally sourced and seasonal food is a distinguishing feature of Michelin-starred restaurants. Chefs create menus that showcase the richness of the regional terroir while celebrating the flavors and freshness of each season. The origins of food take on a story of their own, taking diners on a gourmet tour of the area's abundance.
5. **Tasting Menus and Culinary Journeys:** Tasting menus, which consist of a series of carefully chosen dishes that unfold like a culinary narrative, are available at many restaurants with Michelin stars. Through a range of tastes, methods, and textures, guests can experience these culinary adventures, which offer a comprehensive investigation of the chef's culinary philosophy.
6. **Architectural Ambiance and Design:** The atmosphere of restaurants with Michelin stars is not limited to the food itself. Cozy surroundings, elegant architecture, and sophisticated design all work together to create an ambiance that enhances the culinary artistry. Eating turns into a multisensory, immersive experience.
7. **Destination Dining and Culinary Tourism:** Michelin-starred restaurants can become into travel destinations in and of themselves, drawing foodies from all over the world. These culinary treasures add to the growing trend of culinary tourism, in which tourists travel the world to enjoy the best dining experiences. Every restaurant with a Michelin star turns becomes a beacon, attracting gourmets searching for unmatched culinary experiences.

Visiting Tips:

Since Michelin-starred restaurants frequently have a small seating capacity, reservations are important.

Investigate the wine pairings that the restaurant's sommelier has recommended to improve your entire dining experience.

Seize the chance to engage with the chefs through open kitchen concepts or chef's tables to get an intimate look at the culinary artistry behind the scenes.

A Michelin-starred meal is an ode to culinary artistry, where great ingredients, inventive cooking methods, and attentive service come together to create a memorable dining experience. Every dining experience becomes a voyage into the realm of culinary perfection, whether you're enjoying the precision of a three-star establishment or discovering the inventiveness of a one-star jewel. Michelin-starred dining is an invitation to explore the pinnacles of culinary inventiveness and lose oneself in a world where every mouthful is a revelation for those looking to enhance their gastronomic adventures.

Chapter 6
Cultural Experiences

West End Shows: London's Theater Scene

The West End, a theatrical destination with a stunning selection of top-notch productions that enthrall audiences worldwide, is tucked away in the cultural center of London. The West End is widely recognised as the epitome of live performance magic, with its historic theaters providing the perfect setting for the world's best performers to tell captivating, thought-provoking, and inspirational tales. Taking a trip with a West End show is more than just seeing a show; it's an event where stage charm and dramatic skill combine to create theatrical memories that last a lifetime.

1. The West End Legacy: The West End has a long history, and its famous theaters—the London Palladium, the Theatre Royal Drury Lane, and the Royal Opera House—stand as enduring testaments to the splendor of theater. The theater has evolved in these hallowed halls, from Shakespearean plays to modern musical extravaganzas.

2. A Diverse Theatrical Palette: The West End is home to a wide variety of theatrical offerings, ranging from avant-garde performances and Broadway-style musicals to classic plays and contemporary tragedies. Every taste is catered for in the selection of performances, so theatergoers, whether new to the art or seasoned experts, are sure to discover a show that suits their tastes.

3. Musical Extravaganzas: The West End is home to spectacular productions of musical theater that combine compelling stories with jaw-dropping performances. From modern hits like "Hamilton" to timeless favorites like "The Phantom of the Opera," the West End's musical repertory consistently raises the bar for theatrical brilliance.

4. Theatrical Icons and Emerging Talent: The West End provides a platform for both established performers and up-and-coming artists, fostering a vibrant environment where established performers and up-and-coming stars coexist. Because of the high standard of performances on the

West End, viewers are certain to see the pinnacle of theatrical talent, with every performer contributing nuance and realism to their parts.

5. Cultural Landmarks: West End theaters are more than just places to see shows; they are historical cultural icons. The elaborate exteriors and sumptuous interiors of these architecturally stunning theaters provide an additional element of magic to the theatrical experience. A trip down memory lane and a celebration of the stage's timeless enchantment unfold when you see a West End production.

6. The West End Experience: A trip to a West End show is an experience in itself, even beyond the performances. The atmosphere of expectancy before the curtain rises, the audience's collective gasps and cheers, and the conversations that follow the performance at local cafes all add to the immersive quality of the West End experience. Theaters are more than just places to perform; they are gathering places where common stories are brought to life.

7. Accessibility and Inclusivity: The West End is dedicated to inclusion and accessibility, and many of its theaters offer amenities to visitors with impairments. A friendly atmosphere where a wide range of audiences may enjoy the delights of live performance is fostered by the variety of productions offered, guaranteeing that there is something for everyone.

Visiting Tips:

Make reservations well in advance, especially for well-attended shows.

For a more laid-back and affordable theater experience, consider matinee performances.

Get a taste of the lively theater neighborhood before or after the show by dining at one of the neighboring cafés or restaurants.

The West End is proof of the timeless appeal of live theater, where the stage's magic never fails to enthrall and captivate. The West End offers a unique window into the world of theatrical arts, whether exploring the rich fabric of historic tragedies, being mesmerized by musical extravaganza, or seeing the rise of new theatrical voices. Seeing a play in the West End is more than simply a night out; it's an invitation to immerse yourself in London's rich theatrical history, where the allure of narrative comes to life under the glow of the stage lights.

Museums and Galleries: Art and History

London's cultural environment is replete with galleries and museums, each serving as a haven for history buffs and art aficionados alike. The city's museums and galleries, which range from well-known establishments to undiscovered treasures, construct a story spanning ages and provide an engrossing voyage through the spheres of invention, creativity, and human achievement. Discovering London's cultural establishments is more than just a trip there—an it's immersion into the rich history and artistic legacy that shape the city's identity.

1. **The British Museum: A Global Odyssey:** The British Museum, which has an enormous collection spanning countries and millennia, is a monument to human history. Every item, from the Elgin Marbles to the Rosetta Stone, narrates a tale of cultures, civilizations, and the advancement of human understanding. The Great Court is a symbol of world heritage because of its magnificent architecture and the museum's dedication to cross-cultural interchange.
2. **The National Gallery: Masters on Display:** A refuge for art enthusiasts, The National Gallery is tucked away near Trafalgar Square and features masterpieces from the 13th to the 19th centuries. Its walls are covered in paintings by Rembrandt, Van Gogh, and Leonardo da Vinci, which provide an immersive tour

through the development of European painting. The classic atmosphere of the museum makes it easier to appreciate every color scheme and brushstroke.

3. **Tate Modern: Contemporary Expression:** Tucked away along the Thames in a decommissioned power plant, Tate Modern is a champion of modern art. Its huge Turbine Hall is home to imposing installations, while its galleries display pieces by contemporary artists. Picasso's groundbreaking works and provocative installations notwithstanding, Tate Modern is a dynamic canvas that captures the fluctuating terrain of artistic expression.

4. **The Victoria and Albert Museum: Artistic Eclecticism:** The Victoria and Albert Museum—more affectionately referred to as the V&A—celebrates diversity in the arts. The museum's varied holdings cover eras and cultures and range from fashion and design to sculpture and decorative arts. Every visit is an investigation into the beauty hidden in the commonplace because of its dedication to presenting the relationship between art and daily life.

5. **The Natural History Museum: Nature's Wonders:** The Natural History Museum, a cathedral of natural wonders, welcomes guests to ponder the glories of the natural world. The museum arouses wonder and interest with its exhibits, which range from the massive Diplodocus skeleton in the Hintze Hall to the captivating diamonds in the Vault Gallery. Explore Earth's biodiversity in a family-friendly environment with interactive displays and educational exhibitions.

6. **The Science Museum: Innovation Unleashed:** The Science Museum brings the wonders of science and technology to life, serving as a playground for creativity and exploration. A journey through humankind's desire for knowledge and advancement, the museum features objects from space exploration to early steam engines. All ages are captivated by interactive exhibitions that make science's marvels approachable and fascinating.

7. **The National Portrait Gallery: Faces of History:** Through portraiture, the National Portrait Gallery vividly depicts historical events. The faces that formed the story of the British Isles are captured in the gallery's collection, which includes everything from rulers to literary titans. Every portrait offers a glimpse into

the characters and narratives that have had a profound impact on the political and cultural scene.

Visiting Tips:

Sort important exhibits first, but make space for unexpected finds as well.

Look for activities, guided tours, and special exhibitions on the websites of the museums.

For a more personal encounter, think about going during off-peak times.

London's galleries and museums are living archives that chronicle the evolution of humankind through time, not only stores of things and relics. Every institution adds to the city's cultural mix with its distinct personality and holdings. Discovering these cultural treasures is a call to investigate the past, accept the present, and ponder the infinite possibilities of the future.

Music Scene: From Classical to Contemporary

London's music scene is a symphony of harmonizing melodies that echoes the dynamic rhythms of cultural fusions, the throbbing pulses of contemporary genres, and the various melodies of classical works. Via intimate settings and ancient concert halls, the city serves as a stage for a wide range of musical events. Getting involved in London's music scene means more than just going to shows; it means taking a trip through the diverse range of musical expression that permeates this vibrant city.

1. **Royal Albert Hall: The Epitome of Elegance:** Situated in the center of South Kensington, the Royal Albert Hall is a model of sophistication and magnificence. From rock concerts and contemporary music events to classical concerts and operas, this legendary venue presents a wide variety of acts. For those who love music, its magnificent domed structure and top-notch acoustics provide an immersive experience.
2. **The Barbican Centre: A Cultural Hub:** A refuge for culture, the Barbican Centre honours music in all its manifestations. The Barbican's varied schedule, which features everything from avant-

garde concerts to traditional orchestras, demonstrates its dedication to expanding the possibilities for musical expression. The center is a vibrant hub for musical exploration thanks to its contemporary architecture and multipurpose areas.

3. **The Jazz Scene in Soho: Timeless Vibes:** For many years, Soho's lively ambiance and historic alleyways have served as the hub of London's jazz scene. Small jazz venues such as Ronnie Scott's Jazz Club have been the scene for historic shows that draw both fans and novices. The classic atmosphere of Soho's jazz clubs offers a haven for those looking for the soulful notes of this very urban genre.

4. **The O2 Arena: Epicenter of Entertainment:** Located on the Greenwich Peninsula, the O2 Arena is a massive entertainment venue that presents a wide range of musical genres and holds mega-concerts. With its enormous stage and cutting-edge amenities, the O2 Arena offers audiences an experience that is larger than life for both famous rock bands and global pop sensations.

5. **Camden's Alternative Sound: Subcultural Resonance:** Camden Town is a melting pot of musical expression, well-known for its alternative and subcultural influences. Legends like Pink Floyd and The Doors have performed at the renowned Roundhouse. Camden's diverse blend of alternative, punk, and indie music genres never fails to draw in music lovers looking to get a taste of London's underground scene.

6. **Southbank Centre: Riverside Serenades:** The Southbank Centre, nestled along the Thames, is a cultural complex that embraces diverse musical genres. From classical concerts at the Royal Festival Hall to experimental sounds at the Queen Elizabeth Hall, the Southbank Centre fosters a dynamic environment where the river's serenade accompanies the melodies within.

7. **Music Festivals Across the City: A Sonic Kaleidoscope:** London hosts an array of music festivals throughout the year, transforming parks, squares, and venues into sonic playgrounds. From the eclectic sounds of the Notting Hill Carnival to the indie vibes of All Points East, these festivals amplify the city's diverse musical offerings, bringing together artists and audiences in a celebration of sound.

Visiting Tips:

For more intimate and distinctive musical experiences, check out smaller, independent venues.

Look through the local listings to find free events taking place all across the city, such as pop-up concerts.

Attend open mic evenings to get a taste of the local music scene and meet up-and-coming artists.

The music scene in London is a celebration of ethnic diversity, a kaleidoscope of sounds, and a fusion of genres. The city's musical landscape encourages exploration and discovery, whether one chooses to embrace the raw intensity of alternative venues or relish the polished notes of ancient concert halls. London's music scene is more than simply a collection of songs; it is a vibrant, living example of how music has the ability to bridge divides and bring people together.

Literary London: Bookish Hotspots

London, a city rich in literary heritage, is a maze of bookish delights where old and new stories resound in bookstores, libraries, and landmarks. Discovering Literary London is more than just taking a walk down the streets; it's an engaging trip into the world of words, stories, and the ongoing legacy of literature. From the haunts of literary giants to the hidden gems loved by bibliophiles.

1. **The British Library: Literary Treasures:** Nestled in a bibliophile's paradise, the British Library holds an immense collection of literary relics. The library has a collection that spans decades and continents, including the original Shakespeare manuscripts and the Magna Carta. A revolving exhibition of rare books, literary maps, and manuscripts that trace the development of written language is unveiled by the Sir John Ritblat Gallery.
2. **Shakespeare's Globe: The Bard's Stage:** Shakespeare's Globe Theatre, a living monument to the Bard's timeless words, lies tucked away along the banks of the Thames. Shakespeare's plays are performed at the Globe, which recreates the ambiance of an

Elizabethan playhouse. It welcomes visitors to enjoy the ageless wonder of live theater in an evocative setting steeped in history.
3. **The Charles Dickens Museum: A Writer's Haven:** Visit Charles Dickens' former home, which is now the Charles Dickens Museum, and immerse yourself in his world. This literary sanctuary, which is situated in Bloomsbury, lets guests view the writer's belongings, manuscripts, and the actual rooms where some of his best-loved books were written. One of the greatest storytellers in literature, the museum takes visitors on a journey through his life and times.
4. **Daunt Books: Literary Exploration:** For readers who are interested in exploring literature, Daunt Books is a sanctuary with its skylights and galleries made of Edwardian oak. Daunt Books, a travel literature specialist, provides a carefully chosen assortment that reflects the spirit of exploration and adventure. Book lovers will find the Edwardian elegance of the Marylebone branch to be a captivating setting.
5. **The London Review Bookshop: Literary Conversations:** Tucked away in Bloomsbury, The London Review Bookshop is more than just a bookshop—a it's meeting place for writers. Come to conversations, book launches, and author appearances in our little independent bookstore. Readers with sophisticated tastes will find great pleasure in the well chosen selection of novels, which mirrors the literary preferences of the London Review of Books.
6. **Keats House: Poetic Serenity:** Embrace the poetic serenity of Keats House in Hampstead, where John Keats composed some of his most celebrated works. The tranquil surroundings, coupled with the museum's collection of Keats's personal belongings, create an atmosphere that invites reflection on the beauty and transience of life, echoing the sentiments of Keats's poetry.
7. **Persephone Books: Rediscovering Forgotten Classics:** Persephone Books, nestled in Bloomsbury, is a literary oasis dedicated to rediscovering forgotten classics, particularly those written by female authors. The charming shop showcases a collection of neglected gems, each adorned with distinctive gray covers. Persephone Books is a celebration of women's voices and a treasure trove for readers seeking unique literary finds.

Visiting Tips:

Discover the bookish secrets of London by taking one of the literary walking tours offered there.

Participate in literary festivals and celebrations honoring writers, literature, and the written word.

Join discussion and book clubs in your community to introduce other book lovers to the pleasure of reading.

Literary London is a live example of the transformational power of words and tales, not just a collection of bookish hotspots. London welcomes readers to immerse themselves in the literary tapestry that interweaves the history, present, and future of written expression, from the sacred halls of the British Library to the cozy booksellers that line the city's streets. Discovering Literary London takes readers on a trip into the core of narrative, where every turn of the page and every word said becomes a celebration of the timeless allure of books.

Festivals and Events: Celebrating Diversity

A celebration of diversity, London's vivid tapestry of festivals and events brings cultures, traditions, and artistic expressions together in a harmonic kaleidoscope. The city's calendar is packed with exciting events that bring people together, encourage creativity, and highlight the diversity of the human experience, from vibrant parades to music festivals. Experiencing London's festivals entails more than just going to events; it involves taking part in a group celebration that cuts across boundaries and celebrates diversity in all of its forms.

1. **Notting Hill Carnival: Caribbean Rhythms and Colors:** A vibrant celebration of Caribbean culture, the Notting Hill Carnival turns West London's streets into a riot of hues and beats. The carnival is a happy celebration of London's Caribbean community and a monument to the city's inclusivity, with its colorful costumes, exuberant parades, and addictive steel drum beats.
2. **Diwali on the Square: Festival of Lights:** During the yearly Diwali on the Square event, Trafalgar Square is illuminated by the

brightness of Diwali, the Festival of Lights. The celebration invites individuals of all backgrounds to join in the celebrations and embrace the spirit of light, joy, and cross-cultural interchange. It features traditional Indian dance, music, and cuisine.

3. **Thames Festival: A Riverside Extravaganza:** London's famous riverbanks are transformed into a lively display of performance, music, and art during the Thames Festival. The event unites many communities to celebrate the creative energy that runs along the Thames, embodying the city's dynamic vitality. Events include illuminated night parades and riverbank performances.

4. **Pride in London: LGBTQ+ Celebration:** Pride in London stands as a powerful celebration of LGBTQ+ identity, love, and equality. The annual parade, vibrant with rainbow colors, winds its way through the heart of the city, culminating in Trafalgar Square. The event is a testament to London's commitment to diversity, inclusivity, and the ongoing journey toward acceptance and understanding.

5. **London Film Festival: Cinematic Diversity:** The London Film Festival is a grand cinematic event that honors the variety of narratives presented on large screens. The festival, which presents films from all around the world, invites performers, directors, and moviegoers to participate in an international dialogue about the ability of narrative to promote understanding and overcome cultural divides.

6. **Thames Rockets: New Year's Eve Fireworks Cruise:** Take part in the Thames Rockets New Year's Eve Fireworks Cruise to ring in the new year from a different angle. Take a boat ride on the Thames to see the amazing fireworks show against the backdrop of London's famous monuments. The occasion celebrates a happy beginning to the year and the inclusive and communal attitude of the city.

7. **Southbank Centre's Africa Utopia: Showcasing African Culture:** The Southbank Center is home to Africa Utopia, a festival honoring the vibrant and varied cultures of Africa. The event promotes cross-cultural understanding and communication by exploring the traditional and modern aspects of African identity through song, dance, art, and discussions.

Visiting Tips:

To make sure you can attend particular activities, make advance plans and review the festival program.

Seize the chance to sample the variety of foods that are served during ethnic festivals.

Interact with nearby communities to learn more about the significance of each holiday.

The celebration of the various manifestations of human culture, acceptance of diversity, and promotion of inclusivity are all embodied in London's festivals and events. Every occasion is a lively chapter in the shared story of London's identity, beckoning residents and guests to join in the joyful celebrations that bring people from all walks of life together. By taking part in London's festivals, one may actively celebrate the rich diversity that characterizes our global metropolis rather than merely watching it from a distance.

Chapter 7
Practical Tips and Local Insights

Accommodation Options: From Luxury to Budget

London, a city that skillfully combines the old and the new, has a wide range of lodging choices to suit the tastes and budgets of every visitor. The city offers a variety of lodging options, from luxurious 5-star hotels to comfortable, affordable hostels, so guests can always find a place to call home. Examining London's lodging alternatives is more than simply figuring out where to stay; it's also about figuring out the ideal starting point for a trip of adventure and discovery across this energetic city.

1. **The Ritz London: Timeless Elegance:** Nestled in the heart of Mayfair, The Ritz London stands as an epitome of timeless elegance and luxury. With its iconic architecture and opulent interiors, this five-star hotel has been welcoming royalty and discerning travelers since 1906. The Ritz offers lavish rooms, exquisite dining experiences, and impeccable service, making it a haven for those seeking the epitome of sophistication.
2. **The Savoy: Art Deco Grandeur:** Situated on the Strand, The Savoy has both historical significance and Art Deco grandeur. This opulent hotel with views of the Thames offers exquisite accommodations, fine dining options, and top-notch amenities.

For those looking for sophisticated elegance, the Savoy's historic history paired with its contemporary amenities offer an unmatched experience.
3. **Airbnb Stays: Local Immersion:** Airbnb provides a wide range of lodging alternatives, from stylish apartments to quaint townhouses, for people looking for a more customized and local experience. When guests stay at an Airbnb, they can get a unique perspective of the city and can fully immerse themselves in London's districts, uncovering hidden gems and enjoying the hospitality of local hosts.
4. **The Shard's Shangri-La Hotel: Sky-High Splendor:** For a stay with a view, the Shangri-La Hotel at The Shard offers sky-high splendor and breathtaking panoramas of London's skyline. Located within the iconic Shard skyscraper, this luxury hotel provides elegant accommodations, Michelin-starred dining, and an infinity pool with unparalleled vistas, creating a memorable and elevated experience.
5. **Premier Inn: Comfort and Affordability:** Travelers on a tight budget often choose Premier Inn because of its comfort and reasonable prices. These hotels, which have multiple sites throughout the city, provide free Wi-Fi, spotless, comfy rooms, and on-site eating options. Because of its dedication to providing high-quality service, Premier Inn is a dependable option for a relaxing stay.
6. **YHA London St Pancras: Hostel Experience:** Conveniently located close to King's Cross, YHA London St Pancras offers hostel accommodations for people on a budget and those looking for a sociable atmosphere. With its affordable pricing, communal areas, and dormitory-style accommodations, YHA provides an affordable way to explore the city and meet other tourists.
7. **The Hoxton, Shoreditch: Chic Boutique Vibes:** The Hoxton in Shoreditch is a modern area that exudes elegant boutique atmosphere and modern decor. With its chic accommodations, colorful lobby areas, and energetic ambience, the hotel is a favorite among the trendy set. The Hoxton stands out for its dedication to offering a distinctive and fashionable experience.

Visiting Tips:

- Consider the location's proximity to attractions and public transportation when choosing accommodation.
- Check for special offers, loyalty programs, or package deals offered by hotels for potential discounts.
- Read reviews and guest feedback on various booking platforms to ensure a comfortable stay.

Travelers can choose from a wide variety of lodging alternatives in London, making it easy for them to locate the ideal starting point for seeing this vibrant city. London offers a diverse range of lodging options that enhance the whole trip experience. These options include staying in luxurious historic places, booking local experiences through Airbnb, or experiencing the friendly atmosphere of hostels. Every type of lodging, from the opulence of historic hotels to the allure of boutique stays, contributes to the story of comfort and exploration in the center of London.

Navigating Public Transportation

Getting around London's vast public transport network is essential for making the most of your time and money while visiting. Knowing the ropes of public transportation, from the recognizable red double-decker buses to the vast Underground system, improves the whole travel experience. Learning how to use public transit in London is about more than just getting where you're going; it's about becoming completely absorbed in the city and fusing with its dynamic energy.

1. **London Underground (Tube): The Lifeline:** The Tube, also referred to as the London Underground, is the city's lifeline since it connects various neighborhoods quickly and effectively. The Tube is the best option for short and long distance travel because it has a broad network with 11 lines. Learn the zones on the Tube map, become familiar with the route beneath London's busy streets, and relish this unique experience.
2. **Double-Decker Buses: Scenic Routes:** In addition to being a useful form of transportation, London's red double-decker buses provide visitors a picturesque perspective of the city. The famous Routemaster buses lend a nostalgic touch to the trip, and the vast

bus network reaches places that the Underground does not serve. When boarding buses, utilize an Oyster card or contactless payment methods.
3. **Overground and DLR: Connecting Neighborhoods:** In addition to the Tube system, the London Overground and Docklands Light Railway (DLR) interconnect communities and offer easy access to locations outside of the city center. Particularly in East London, the automated DLR and the orange trains of the Overground are effective modes of transportation.
4. **Oyster Card: Seamless Travel:** For smooth rides on public transit, a traveler's best buddy is the Oyster card. Save money on fares when compared to purchasing paper tickets by loading credit onto the card, tapping in and out at stations, and so on. In addition to the Tube, buses, trams, the DLR, London Overground, and certain National Rail services within London, the Oyster card is accepted anywhere.
5. **River Bus Services: Scenic Waterways:** Explore London from a different perspective by utilizing the River Bus services along the Thames. Connecting key piers, these boats offer a unique and scenic mode of transport. River Bus services are especially convenient for reaching attractions along the riverbanks.
6. **Trams: South London Connections:** Trams provide efficient transportation in South London, connecting neighborhoods like Croydon and Wimbledon. The Tramlink network offers a practical way to navigate areas where traditional train or Tube services might be less accessible.
7. **Walking and Cycling: Healthy Commute:** London's compact city center makes walking an enjoyable and practical option for short distances. Embrace the city's bike-friendly initiatives by using Santander Cycles, colloquially known as Boris Bikes, for a healthy and eco-friendly commute. Numerous cycling lanes and bike-sharing stations make cycling an accessible option.

Visiting Tips:

- **Contactless Payment:** Embrace the convenience of contactless payment methods, such as contactless cards or mobile payment options like Apple Pay and Google Pay. This makes transactions seamless, especially on public transportation.

- **Travel Apps:** Download travel apps like Citymapper, TfL (Transport for London), and Uber to navigate the city more efficiently. These apps provide real-time updates, service disruptions, and optimal routes for your journey.
- **Visitor Oyster Card:** Consider purchasing a Visitor Oyster card, a pre-loaded travel smart card designed for tourists. It offers discounted fares compared to buying individual tickets and can be used on various modes of public transportation.
- **Tube Etiquette:** Familiarize yourself with Tube etiquette. Stand on the right side of escalators to allow others to pass, let passengers alight before boarding, and be mindful of peak travel times to avoid overcrowding.
- **Off-Peak Travel:** Opt for off-peak travel times when possible, especially on the Tube and buses. This not only ensures a more comfortable journey but may also save you money, as off-peak fares are often lower.
- **Walking Tours:** Explore the city on foot by joining walking tours. Many companies offer guided tours that take you through historic neighborhoods, iconic landmarks, and hidden gems. Walking tours provide insights and stories that may not be found in guidebooks.
- **Museum Passes:** If you plan to visit multiple museums and attractions, consider purchasing a London Pass or specific museum passes. These passes often provide skip-the-line access and can be cost-effective, especially if you intend to explore several cultural institutions.
- **Local Cuisine Exploration:** Venture beyond traditional British fare and explore the diverse culinary scene in London. Visit food markets like Borough Market for a variety of international cuisines and street food. Don't miss the chance to try dishes from different cultures.
- **Free Attractions:** Take advantage of London's numerous free attractions. Many museums, including the British Museum and the National Gallery, offer free entry to their permanent collections. Enjoying parks, like Hyde Park and Regent's Park, is also a cost-free way to experience the city.
- **Public Parks:** Enjoy the tranquility of London's public parks. Hyde Park, Regent's Park, and Greenwich Park are just a few

examples where you can relax, have a picnic, or enjoy outdoor activities away from the bustling city streets.
- **Local Events:** Check local event calendars for festivals, markets, and special events happening during your visit. London hosts a variety of cultural, music, and food festivals throughout the year, providing opportunities to immerse yourself in the local scene.
- **Emergency Services:** Familiarize yourself with emergency contact numbers and the location of the nearest hospitals and pharmacies. London has a well-established emergency services system, and it's good to be prepared with necessary information.
- **Weather Preparedness:** Be prepared for London's unpredictable weather. Pack layers, including a waterproof jacket or umbrella, as rain showers can occur at any time. Check the weather forecast before heading out for the day.
- **Local Markets:** Explore the diverse markets across London, such as Camden Market, Portobello Road Market, and Spitalfields Market. These markets offer unique shopping experiences, artisanal products, and a chance to interact with local vendors.
- **Respect Local Customs:** Be mindful of local customs and cultural nuances. London is a multicultural city, and respecting diversity is key to a positive experience. Follow local customs when entering places of worship, attending events, and interacting with locals.

By incorporating these tips into your travel plans, you'll be well-equipped to make the most of your time in London and create lasting memories in this vibrant and dynamic city.

Mastering the art of navigating London's public transportation system opens up a world of exploration and discovery. From the efficient Tube network to the iconic red buses, each mode of transport becomes a part of the urban tapestry, offering a dynamic and diverse way to experience the city's vibrant energy. Whether gliding along the Thames on a River Bus or weaving through historic streets on a double-decker bus, navigating public transportation in London is not just a means to an end; it's an integral part of the London adventure.

Shopping in London: From High-End to Vintage

London has a wide variety of retail experiences to suit every taste and style, making shopping there a delightful excursion. The city's shopping scene reflects its vibrant and multicultural nature, from the opulent boutiques of Bond Street to the unique vintage shops in Shoreditch. Discovering London's shopping areas is more than simply buying stuff; it's also about immersing yourself in the newest styles, finding one-of-a-kind items, and traveling across the city's diverse array of stores.

1. **Bond Street: Luxury Haven:** Known for its sophistication and elegance, Bond Street is a posh shopping area that is home to the flagship stores of premium brands and well-known designers. For individuals searching for the height of exclusivity and luxury, Bond Street is a sanctuary, home to renowned fashion houses and fine jewelry retailers.
2. **Oxford Street: High Street Mecca:** One of the busiest shopping avenues in Europe, Oxford Street is dotted with flagship locations for well-known high street retailers. This busy street is a haven for anyone looking for the newest trends at a range of price ranges because it has a wide selection of clothing, cosmetics, and home goods.
3. **Covent Garden: Unique Boutiques and Markets:** Covent Garden is a bustling neighborhood that expertly combines modern flair with old charm. Discover the distinctive shops on the Piazza, and don't miss the Apple Market, where designers and painters display their works. It's ideal to find unique goods and take in street entertainment in Covent Garden.
4. **Carnaby Street: Trendsetting Style:** Known for being the epicenter of the Swinging Sixties, Carnaby Street still sets trends in fashion. Modern brands, iconic stores, and individual boutiques may be found in this pedestrian-only district. Explore the newest trends and lose yourself in Carnaby's artistic atmosphere.
5. **Camden Market: Alternative Finds:** Vintage clothing, one-of-a-kind accessories, and handcrafted goods can be found in abundance at Camden Market, which is well-known for its alternative and eccentric products. Discover the market's intricate network of stands, boutiques, and small stores, and get a taste of Camden's bohemian vibe.

6. **Portobello Road Market: Vintage Paradise:** Notting Hill's Portobello Road Market, known for its unique stalls and antique stores, is a vintage haven. Look through a variety of interesting discoveries, such as vintage apparel and antique artifacts. The market is made more appealing by its colorful stores and lively ambiance.
7. **Shoreditch: Quirky and Independent:** A variety of unique and independent stores can be found in Shoreditch, an artsy and fashionable district. Investigate concept boutiques, avant-garde fashion stores, and vintage shops. Fashion fans seeking individualistic trends find Shoreditch to be a hotspot due to its unique blend of creativity and commerce.

Visiting Tips:

Weekday shopping trips are preferable if you want to have a more laid-back atmosphere.

Look for seasonal discounts, particularly in January and July when shopping is most popular.

Savor the variety of London's neighborhoods for unique retail experiences.

London offers a vibrant, varied shopping experience that suits a wide range of interests and inclinations. London's shopping areas invite you to experience the flair and creativity of the city, whether you're wandering along Bond Street's opulent boutiques, perusing the vintage treasures of Portobello Road Market, or losing yourself in the avant-garde fashion scene of Shoreditch. Every shopping destination is a new chapter in the dynamic story of London's fashion scene, where the newest styles harmoniously coexist with historical favorites.

Health and Safety Tips for Travelers

Ensuring your health and safety is a priority when traveling, and London, like any major city, requires certain precautions. Here are health and safety tips for travelers visiting London:

Health Tips:

1. Travel Insurance:
   - Before embarking on your journey to London, secure comprehensive travel insurance that covers medical expenses, trip cancellations, and emergency evacuations. Confirm the details of your coverage and carry a copy of your policy.
2. Healthcare System:
   - Familiarize yourself with the UK's National Health Service (NHS), which provides healthcare services. Keep in mind that emergency medical assistance is available by dialing 999. Understand the services offered by NHS and locate the nearest hospitals or medical facilities.
3. Vaccinations:
   - Check with your healthcare provider to ensure you are up-to-date on routine vaccinations. Additionally, inquire about any specific vaccinations recommended for travel to the UK. Having proper vaccinations safeguards your health during your stay.
4. Prescription Medications:
   - If you are on prescription medication, ensure you have an ample supply to cover the duration of your trip. Pack medications in their original packaging, clearly labeled with your name and dosage instructions. Carry a copy of your prescription and, if possible, a letter from your doctor explaining your medical condition.
5. Medical Facilities:
   - Identify hospitals, clinics, and pharmacies near your accommodation. Prominent hospitals in central London include St Thomas' and University College Hospital. Keep a list of emergency contacts, including local healthcare providers.
6. Health Precautions:
   - Adopt good hygiene practices, including regular handwashing with soap and water. Carry a small bottle of hand sanitizer for instances when access to soap is limited. Be conscious of your health, especially during flu seasons, and consider getting a flu shot before traveling.

Safety Tips:

1. Emergency Services:
   - Memorize the emergency contact number, 999, for immediate assistance from police, fire, and medical services. For non-emergencies, such as reporting a crime, contact the police at 101. Save important numbers in your phone for quick access.
2. Awareness of Surroundings:
   - Maintain situational awareness, particularly in crowded places, tourist attractions, and public transportation. Beware of pickpockets and keep your belongings secure. Consider using a money belt or a crossbody bag to deter theft.
3. Public Transportation Safety:
   - Follow safety guidelines on public transportation. Be cautious when navigating crowded areas, and remain vigilant against potential risks. Familiarize yourself with emergency procedures and exits on public transport.
4. Traffic and Pedestrian Safety:
   - Since traffic moves on the left side in the UK, always look right before crossing the road. Utilize designated pedestrian crossings, obey traffic signals, and be cautious of cyclists and motorists.
5. Safe Areas:
   - London is generally safe, but like any major city, it has areas with varying safety levels. Research neighborhoods before your visit, and exercise caution, especially in less familiar areas. Stick to well-lit streets at night and consider using reputable transportation services.
6. Cybersecurity:
   - Protect your personal information online by using secure Wi-Fi connections, avoiding public computers for sensitive tasks, and employing a virtual private network (VPN) for added security. Be cautious when using public Wi-Fi networks to prevent unauthorized access to your devices.
7. Weather Preparedness:
   - London's weather can be unpredictable, so pack clothing suitable for varying conditions. Include an umbrella, waterproof jacket, and layers to stay comfortable, especially during seasonal changes.

8. Fire Safety:
   - Prioritize fire safety by familiarizing yourself with escape routes in your accommodation. Abide by no-smoking regulations and exercise caution with fire sources. Follow safety instructions provided in your accommodation.
9. Cultural Sensitivity:
   - Respect local customs and cultural norms. London is a diverse city with various communities, so be mindful of your behavior in religious or cultural sites. Dress modestly when appropriate, and seek guidance if unsure about local customs.
10. Emergency Contacts:
    - Keep a list of important contacts, including the contact information for your country's embassy or consulate in London. Store local emergency service numbers, such as the non-emergency police line (101), in your phone for quick reference.

By incorporating these health and safety tips into your travel preparations, you can prioritize your well-being and enjoy a secure and enriching experience during your time in London.

Sustainable Travel: Responsible Tourism in London

Accepting sustainable travel methods is crucial for responsible tourism in London, a city renowned for its lively urban life, rich history, and diverse culture. Traveling sustainably guarantees that tourists have a beneficial influence on the environment and nearby communities. Travelers may contribute to the well-being of London and its residents by using responsible tourism practices, which range from eco-friendly lodging to thoughtful transit choices. This article looks at how tourists can experience sustainable travel while taking in London's vibrant city life.

1. Eco-Friendly Accommodations:

   - Select lodgings that have green programs or certifications. Seek out lodging establishments that engage in water conservation, waste reduction, and energy conservation initiatives. Many London hotels engage in eco-friendly activities, offering guests who care about the environment a responsible stay.

2. Sustainable Transportation:

- Opt for public transportation, cycling, or walking to explore London. The city's extensive public transport network, including buses and the Underground, is efficient and minimizes the environmental impact. Consider using bike-sharing schemes or walking tours to further reduce your carbon footprint.

3. Responsible Sightseeing:

- Make it a priority to visit sites that use ethical and sustainable processes. Several famous sites in London, such as the British Museum and the Tower of London, have adopted environmentally conscious programs. Encourage companies that make sustainability a top priority in their operations.

4. Local and Sustainable Dining:

- Investigate eateries and restaurants that prioritize sustainable and local sources. Farm-to-table eating alternatives are available in London because to the city's diversified culinary culture, which also lessens the environmental effect of food transportation by supporting local farmers. For a more sustainable dining experience, think about choosing vegetarian or vegan options.

5. Reduce Single-Use Plastics:

- To lessen your dependency on single-use plastics, carry a reusable water bottle that you can refill at approved water stations. The Refill campaign is supported by a large number of London's parks, eateries, and attractions, making it simple to stay hydrated without adding to the city's plastic waste.

6. Engage in Community-Based Tourism:

- Engage in constructive interactions with local communities by taking part in community-based tourist initiatives. Think about going on neighborhood markets, doing guided tours with locals, or going to cultural activities that directly improve the quality of life for the locals.

7. Waste Reduction:

- Reduce the amount of single-use items you buy and sort recyclables correctly to reduce waste. Consider how to dispose of waste and select items with the least amount of packing. Visitors can support London's recycling efforts by adhering to the city's trash management regulations.

8. Respect Nature in Parks and Gardens:

- Respect the environment while you enjoy London's green spots, like Hyde Park or Kew Gardens. Follow any rules that the parks may have established, stay on trails that are specified, and don't trash. Take part in peaceful pursuits like nature walks and bird viewing to avoid upsetting the local fauna.

9. Support Responsible Tourism Initiatives:

- Choose tour operators and travel agencies that prioritize responsible and sustainable tourism. Support initiatives that contribute to local conservation, community development, and cultural preservation.

10. Cultural Sensitivity: - Respect local customs and traditions. Learn about the cultural heritage of London and engage with local communities in a respectful manner. Support initiatives that aim to preserve and celebrate London's cultural diversity.

11. Offset Your Carbon Footprint: - Consider offsetting your travel-related carbon emissions by supporting carbon offset projects. Many organizations offer carbon offset programs that fund initiatives to reduce greenhouse gas emissions and promote sustainability.

12. Stay Informed: - Stay informed about sustainability initiatives and developments in London. Follow local news, participate in community events, and be aware of any campaigns or programs promoting responsible tourism.

By incorporating these sustainable travel practices into your London itinerary, you can enjoy the city's attractions while minimizing your environmental impact and contributing positively to local communities. Responsible tourism not only preserves the beauty of London but also ensures that future generations can continue to enjoy the city's cultural and natural treasures.

Conclusion

A Sustainable Journey through London's Tapestry

It's clear that London's charm goes far beyond its well-known sites and busy streets as we round out this exploration of the city. We have not only learned about new destinations to visit but have also embarked on a voyage of discovery into the core of sustainable tourism, cultural appreciation, and ethical travel.

We found the links that connect London's history, culture, and modernity, weaving through its maze-like neighborhoods. Every chapter presented a different aspect of London, ranging from the majestic Buckingham Palace to the lively Camden Town markets, and from the ancient Tower of London to the tranquil Hyde Park. However, our investigation extended beyond the obvious tourist destinations, exploring the fundamentals of responsible tourism that align with the city's dedication to a sustainable future.

By choosing eco-friendly lodging, ethically navigating the city, giving back to the community, and enjoying sustainable dining options, we were able to enjoy London's abundant offers while leaving as little trace as possible on Earth. Our dedication to cutting back on single-use plastics, promoting community-based travel, and protecting the environment in parks reflected the environmental consciousness of the city.

We learned that sustainability in the kitchen also applies to the food we put on our plates. London's diversified culinary culture offered not just a feast for the senses but also an awareness for ethical and locally sourced ingredients, from farm-to-table dining to embracing vegetarian and vegan options.

We understood the value of being sensitive to cultural differences, honoring regional traditions, and backing events that highlight London's diverse community as conscientious tourists. Participating in tourism-related community projects and selecting ethical tour operators evolved from simple travel decisions to symbols of our dedication to the sustainability of the places we visit.

With its abundance of attractions and dedication to sustainability, London has provided a backdrop for travel experiences that go above the norm. The city has urged us to take on the role of caretakers of its natural and cultural heritage in addition to visitors. Our environmentally friendly tour of London is evidence that, when done ethically, travel can have a transforming effect and leave a good legacy for the destinations we visit.

Let us take with us the knowledge gained and the experiences created as we bid adieu to London's busy streets, iconic sites, and varied neighborhoods. May the values of sustainable travel, responsible tourism, and a profound respect for the distinctive tales each place has to offer continue to serve as our compass. London has been a gracious host on this voyage, welcoming us to be not just guests but caretakers of its magnificent past with its open arms and rich tapestry.

www.ingramcontent.com/pod-product-compliance
Lightning Source LLC
LaVergne TN
LVHW020140080526
838202LV00048B/3981